GROUNDWORK GUIDES

Empire
James Laxer
Being Muslim
Haroon Siddiqui
Genocide
Jane Springer
Climate Change
Shelley Tanaka

Series Editor
Jane Springer

GROUNDWORK GUIDES

Empire

James Laxer

Groundwood Books
House of Anansi Press

Toronto Berkeley

Groundwood Books / House of Anansi Press
110 Spadina Avenue, Suite 801, Toronto, Ontario M5V 2K4
Distributed in the USA by Publishers Group West
1700 Fourth Street, Berkeley, CA 94710

ONTARIO ARTS COUNCIL
CONSEIL DES ARTS DE L'ONTARIO

We acknowledge for their financial support of our publishing program the Canada Council for the Arts, the Government of Canada through the Book Publishing Industry Development Program (BPIDP) and the Ontario Arts Council. Special thanks to the Ontario Media Development Corporation.

Library and Archives Canada Cataloging in Publication
Laxer, James
Empire / by James Laxer.
(Groundwork Guides)
Includes bibliographical references and index.
ISBN-13: 978-0-88899-706-7 (bound)
ISBN-10: 0-88899-706-X (bound)
ISBN-13: 978-0-88899-707-4 (pbk.)
ISBN-10: 0-88899-707-8 (pbk.)
1. Imperialism. 2. United States–Foreign relations–2001-.
3. United States–Military policy. I. Title. II. Series.
JZ1480.L39 2006   327.7309'051   C2006-902733-1

Printed and bound in Canada

To Julia and Benjamin

Acknowledgments

I am indebted to Patsy Aldana, who came up with the exciting concept for this series of books and proposed this book to me. Once again I am involved in a publishing venture with my good friend Patsy, a delight for me.

Jane Springer has done a wonderful job as editor, making suggestions to improve the structure and flow of the manuscript and honing its details. My literary agent, Jackie Kaiser, as always, has been there with support and encouragement.

Thanks to my partner, Sandy, for allowing yet another project to be a constant presence in our lives.

I am grateful to the team at Groundwood, Nan Froman, Michael Solomon and Sarah Quinn, for the wonderful job they've done with this book and the series. And thanks to Leon Grek for the excellent maps.

Contents

Chapter 1
What Is an Empire?

Empires have existed for thousands of years. Indeed, the first empires came into being at the very dawn of civilization. The imperial form of political and social organization has been one of the most persistent ways to govern societies, and continues to be extremely important in our world at the beginning of the twenty-first century. Because empires take many different forms, a simple working definition is needed at the outset.

An empire exists when one nation, tribe or society exercises long-term domination over one or more external nations, tribes or societies. Through that domination the imperial power, or empire, is able to determine many of the key political, social, economic and cultural outcomes in the dominated society or societies. And that is the critical point — the ability of the empire to determine what happens, the outcomes in the societies under its control, is what distinguishes an empire from other forms of political organization. Those who hold power at the center of an empire typically derive economic benefits, access to important resources, control of militarily strategic territory and other forms of power as a consequence of imperial arrangements.

Typically, we have an image in our minds of an empire as an old-fashioned arrangement under which one power, say Rome or Britain, conquers and occupies the lands of many peoples and rules them from an imperial capital. Without Rome's imperial legions or Britain's navy such an empire could not have existed. Laws made in London or promulgated by the emperor in Rome were enforced across the empire. The Union Jack, the British flag, flew over the territories of the empire. This kind of formal empire has existed many times in different parts of the world. In addition to formal empires, however, there are informal empires. Informal empires — much of the British Empire was informal — exist when the imperial power does not actually annex the territories it dominates. In those territories, there is a local government in place, which may be national or tribal, and in theory, the laws of the imperial power are not in force there.

To prevent the Egyptian government from defaulting on bonds issued on its public debt and held by Europeans, and to secure the Suez Canal, the British military occupied Egypt in 1882, making the country effectively a part of the British Empire. British troops and ships were garrisoned in Egypt. Following the British seizure of control, Egypt was to all intents and purposes ruled by a British appointee whose modest title was "British Agent and Consul-General." In theory, though, Egypt had its own ruler, and to make matters more complicated still, it remained a province in the Ottoman Empire, whose capital was Istanbul. But the Ottoman Empire was in decline and its sultan had no real authority in Egypt. In this case, there was an arrangement in which the old formal imperial power was collapsing, a new national Egyptian government was in place, but the crucial decision-making power lay in the hands of another imperial power, which in theory was not the ruler of the country. Empires, this illustrates, are not as simple as we may have imagined. And they come in many different shapes and sizes.

Today the American Empire is the world's greatest power, universally recognized as the only superpower of our era. It is almost entirely an informal empire and the label "empire" is one that American political leaders never use to describe American global power. While for European states in the past, the word "empire" was positively embraced — as in the cases of the British, French or German empires — for Americans, the word has always had negative connotations. This is because in the American Revolution, the founding fathers of the United States and the patriots they led proclaimed that they were fighting against the British Empire and on behalf of the right, not only of Americans, but of all peoples, to be free of imperial rule. Later in this book, we will return to the case of the United States and make the argument that today there is an American Empire and that its policies determine economic, political, military and cultural outcomes for very large parts of the world.

The first empires came into being with the establishment of the earliest civilizations. We don't know the names of those empires and we have few records of their existence. What we can conclude, however, is that empire came into being alongside another institution with a very long pedigree — slavery. Slavery and empire came into existence in the same historical epoch and for much the same reasons.

In the earliest days of human existence, techniques for gathering food and acquiring shelter were so rudimentary that no surplus of any sort was possible. A small number of people living together in a band could only scrape together enough food to feed themselves. It was perfectly possible for such groups to have enemies, rival bands with whom they fought over a particular habitat. But there was no point for the victors in such squabbles to take the vanquished into slavery. The slaves would only have been able to generate enough food to meet their own needs. But imagine then a very small improvement in food-gathering techniques that would allow, for the first time, the reaping by an individual of more food than he or she could consume. Imagine, therefore, the creation of the very first surplus production as a consequence of human labor. Though the surplus was not large, it opened up the possibility that a privileged few could live off the surplus produced by an enslaved many. It now made sense, as the consequence of a victory over foes, to enslave the survivors rather than simply killing, or in some cases, even eating them.

Slavery was the seminal institution in the launch of civilization, and with it came empire. The surplus production of slaves allowed for the creation of a small privileged class of rulers who could spend their time freed from the most menial kind of labor. The privileged ones could be rulers, warriors or priests. They could even be, at a somewhat later time, thinkers, people with that most valuable of commodities, free time to devote to activities other than the relentless struggle for mere survival.

It is not difficult to see how empire and slavery come into the equation together. As a consequence of a victory in battle of one band, tribe or society over another, whole peoples could be vanquished by the victors. Military victories thus could net slaves for a rising and conquering society. The slaves, therefore, were not merely an underclass, but an alien underclass, members of a defeated society brought within the sway of a nascent imperial power. The first empires, thus established, were doubtless rudimentary affairs and the discovery, if we can call it that, of the benefits of conquest to acquire slave labor, was doubtless made countless times in different parts of the world. Rulers, then and later, were no doubt not particularly pleased to see their rising good fortune

Slavery and Empire

In 1878, Friedrich Engels, Karl Marx's close collaborator, wrote a famous passage establishing the link between the institutions of slavery and empire. Engels advanced the idea that at the dawn of recorded history "production had so far developed that the labour power of a man could now produce more than was necessary" to keep that man alive. To put it another way, human methods had reached the point that a small band of men, women and their offspring could produce a little more than they needed to keep them alive. And that opened the door to a twin revolution.

"Slavery was invented," wrote Engels. "It soon became the predominant form of production among all peoples who were developing beyond the primitive community." By forcing people into slavery, a dominant group of people could acquire additional labor. There were two ways this could be done. Some members of the group or tribe could be compelled to become slaves. But perhaps more likely, the tribe could conquer a neighboring tribe and force its members into slavery. And that conquest established the earliest and most primitive form of empire.

It is hard to resist Engels' conclusion that slavery and empire were conceived together. "Without slavery, no Greek state, no Greek art and science; without slavery, no Roman Empire," he wrote.[1]

attributed to mere conquest and the acquisition of slave labor. The thought, even today, that the rise of civilization was the consequence of slavery and empire is not an attractive one to contemplate.

Thousands of years would pass before these early, or proto, empires would develop into the complex civilizations of which we have an historical record. At the beginning of the twenty-first century, we are much closer in time to the days of the great Roman and Chinese empires than those empires were to the first empires to come into being. The Han Chinese and Roman empires, existing in different parts of the world and overlapping in time, were developmentally far more advanced than the earliest empires that came into being thousands of years before them.

Types of Empire
The Chinese and Roman empires are among the most complex and advanced of the earliest form of empire, which we can call the peasant or slave empire. Three other forms of empire have arisen over the millennia since the days of the Han Chinese and Roman empires.

First came the mercantile empire, an early example of which was the Venetian Empire, which reached its zenith from the twelfth to the fourteenth centuries. The most far-flung of the mercantile empires was that of Spain, which became the world's greatest power from the late fifteenth century to the late seventeenth century. The early British and French empires, whose struggles dominated the eighteenth century, were initially attempts to copy the Spanish Empire.

Mercantile empires were launched in societies that had developed an early form of capitalism. (In capitalism, investors and owners earned profits from enterprises they controlled. Under feudalism, in contrast, aristocrats collected a portion of the produce of the serfs on their lands and those serfs were required, as well, to perform labor for aristocrats.) The goal of mercantile empires was to reap profits from foreign conquests, and bankers and other financiers invested large sums to send Spanish expeditions to the New World in search of gold and silver. Along the way, the Spaniards overthrew mighty indigenous Western Hemisphere empires, the Aztecs, the Maya and the Incas, setting up their own system of imperial rule. The main goal from the start, though, was bullion, to be brought home to Spain in the great galleons that dominated the seas in the days of Spain's empire. Mercantile empires made use of brutal conquests, thievery and the deployment of peasants and slaves to reap their profits.

The next form of empire, the form most common in what was called "the age of imperialism" in the nineteenth and early twentieth centuries, was the capitalist empire. The classic imperialism of the nineteenth century involved an immense campaign by the European powers to annex the as yet unconquered parts of Africa, to seize pieces of Asia and to force China to grant them special powers in regions of that great, but divided and besieged country. The most frenzied period of the land grab took place in the decades after 1870. All the other European powers were following the British example. It was the heyday of Britain, whose rulers boasted that the "sun never set on the British Empire." Maps of the world splashed red across British domains, from Canada to Australia, to large parts of Africa, with the jewel of the whole imperial enterprise the Indian subcontinent. By contrast, the British Isles, small bits of land off the northwestern corner of Europe, the center of it all, were tiny dots of red on a world map. The British and the other empires of the age were carved out by capitalist powers, in the full flush of industrialism and in a threatening new age of militarism.

Scholars, journalists and political leaders alike, during that age, debated whether imperialism was profitable for the imperial powers. Did the cost of governing and securing the colonies outweigh the profits realized in them? Observers produced tables that showed that Britain and the others were spending more on their overseas holdings than they were earning back from them. More important than the numbers on the tables was the fact that the people paying taxes for the governing of the colonies and those profiting from them were, for the most part, not the same people. While the general public paid into the coffers of the state to run the colonies, the sons of aristocrats got most of the top posts in the colonial realms, and great financiers and investors, like Cecil Rhodes in South Africa, made the super profits. For these privileged people, the empires were well worth it.

The sun set on the British and the other great European empires in the decade or two following the end of the Second World War. By the end of the 1960s, the age of imperialism seemed to have come to an end. In the era of the Cold War, two superpowers, with sharply different ideologies, the United States and the Soviet Union, dominated the world. Empire appeared to be a thing of the past.

Under closer scrutiny, however, it was evident that the United States and the Soviet Union were both creating their own empires. The Soviet Union's empire was a regional affair, the fruit of the conquest of Eastern Europe by Soviet armies that drove the Nazis out in the last days of the Second World War. Although Eastern European countries had their own governments, the real power lay in Moscow, and when popular movements in Hungary in 1956 and in Czechoslovakia in 1968 sought to achieve democratic regimes ruled by their own citizens, Soviet tanks rolled in and crushed these popular uprisings. The Soviet Empire lasted until 1989, when the reform-minded regime of Mikhail Gorbachev decided no longer to use force to uphold Soviet power in Eastern Europe.

One by one, the Soviet satellite states rose up in revolutions that were almost entirely peaceful and set up their own governments, free from Moscow's grasp. In 1991, the Soviet Union disintegrated and its constituent republics went their own way as separate states, some more or less democratic, others authoritarian, and still others condemned to years of civil strife. In a very short space of time, an empire that was also a superpower crumbled, not as a result of external conquest, but the victim of its own internal contradictions. The collapse of the Soviet Empire was an illustration in our own time of the fact that great political entities can rise and fall with extraordinary suddenness.

During the decades when the Soviet Union was a superpower, the United States was assembling its own, very different and much larger empire. It was a new kind of empire, the fourth type of empire to be encountered in our inquiry. We can call it a global empire, with both a structure and a global reach unlike that of any of its predecessors. While an important part of the British Empire was informal, in that the Union Jack did not fly over it, the largest part of the empire was formally British territory, directly ruled from London or, in the settler dominions, such as Canada, by a locally elected government that had power over domestic affairs. The American Empire, by contrast, is almost wholly an informal affair. What makes it an empire is that American power — economic, political, military and cultural —

shapes crucial decisions in the countries that fall within the empire. Though American power is decisive, national governments administer the countries, a task the Americans do not perform in the way the British once did throughout most of their empire.

In Chapter 3, we will have much more to say about the American Empire. First though, in the next chapter, we will briefly survey the experience and histories of some other empires in different eras and different parts of the world.

This introductory discussion about empire raises a number of questions we should have in mind as we look more closely at particular empires. Who benefits from empire? While it is obvious that a small and powerful group of people at the center of an imperial power derive enormous benefits from running an empire, do the people as a whole in the imperial center benefit from empire, or do they pay a price? What about the people who live in the colonized parts of the empire? Are they exploited and impoverished as a consequence of empire, or do they benefit from the transmission of economic techniques, investment, culture and political ideas from the imperial center? And finally, having observed that empires have existed throughout recorded history, we need to ask, are they likely to remain a crucial part of the human landscape for the foreseeable future?

Chapter 2
Past Empires

Despite the vast differences among them in power, technique, technology and culture, empires face a set of common problems that have been persistent through the ages. One of the problems that besets virtually all empires is what is called "imperial overstretch." The problem arises from the fact that it requires an outlay of manpower and resources, let's call this blood and treasure, to acquire domination over other peoples and to sustain that domination. How an empire deals with the challenge of imperial overstretch has a great deal to do with how long it can be sustained. As we saw in the first chapter, the Soviet Empire rose and fell in a period of just a few decades.

The Egyptian Empire
An ancient empire that dealt very effectively with the problem of imperial overstretch was the Egyptian Empire. Although it experienced serious crises along the way, the Egyptian Empire managed to sustain itself for

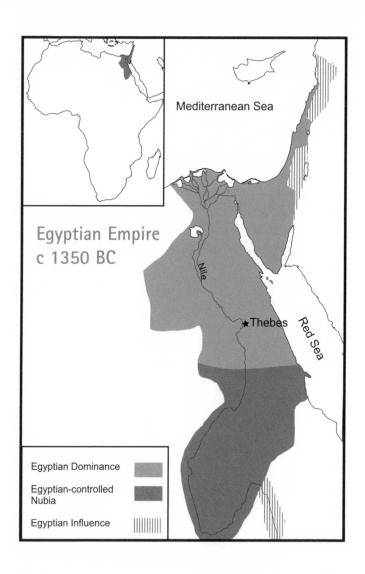

Mediterranean Sea

Egyptian Empire
c 1350 BC

Nile

★Thebes

Red Sea

Egyptian Dominance	
Egyptian-controlled Nubia	
Egyptian Influence	

several thousand years, far longer, for example, than the life spans of the Roman or British empires. Like other early highly developed civilizations, that of the Egyptians arose in a great river valley, the Nile. Along the shores of the Nile River, a ribbon of vegetation and life extended across the pathway of a vast desert. The Egyptian Empire rose along this fertile corridor, hemmed in on the western side by the Sahara Desert and on the eastern side by desert as well, which extended about 160 kilometers (96 miles) further east to the shores of the Red Sea. These rather unique geographical circumstances set the stage for Egyptian historical development. The territory was naturally protected from invaders along its long eastern and western flanks by the desert. It was open to attack only from the north, where the Nile emptied into the Mediterranean, and from the south, by the peoples who lived on the other side of the first Nile cataract, the great waterfall that divided Egypt itself from the peoples to the south in Nubia.

Naturally enough, the rising agricultural society that developed in the Nile Valley depended for its very survival on its control over the fertility of the land. Scholars believe that in the period prior to 3000 BC the Sahara Desert expanded toward the east (deserts have expanded or shrunk in size over the centuries as a consequence of climatic change), pushing people out of the lands on the western edge of the Nile Valley.[1] The consequence was a series of disruptive migrations of people to the east in a search for land that could support them. In this volatile situation, the old order, which had been dominated by local rulers, or regional "strongmen," was overturned by the emergence of a single ruler who managed to impose his authority on the entire country from the Nile Delta in the north to the first Nile cataract in the south. This ruler, conventionally known as Menes, established the Egyptian kingdom that was to survive for nearly three thousand years under the pharaohs. One of the tasks of the central authority was to protect the territory against invasion from the potential weak points in the north and the south. His regime dealt with this risk by building forts at the northern and southern gates of the country.

What made Egypt an empire was the push by its rulers to the south, through military invasions of the territory beyond the first cataract of the Nile. The Egyptian expansion into the land of the Nubians was motivated in large measure by a quest for slave labor, a motivation that was common to other early empires. It is reasonable to characterize this as a "slave-hunting" empire. A slave empire like that of Egypt benefited from the seizure and importation of laborers. The labor of the slaves freed up more Egyptians to become warriors. This was to be the characteristic arrangement on which the slave empires were based.

The Roman Empire
Rome grew to be the greatest of the slave-hunting

empires. It is to Rome that we turn in the W
to find our most potent images of what an e
posed to be like. From the word Caesar has
and Czar, the words used to depict emperors i
and Russia. For well over a thousand years a   ɪan
of the Roman Empire, Rome's highly trained, profes-
sional army — with its famed legions — was the model for
the armies European states wished to establish. Roman
law and Rome's governmental institutions, such as the
Senate, have served as examples from which Western
countries have borrowed over the centuries. Roman
monumental architecture, and the Greek architecture
that so influenced the Romans, has inspired architects of
public buildings and monuments in France, Austria,
modern Italy and the United States. It is no exaggeration
to say that ambitious and powerful leaders from
Charlemagne to Napoleon, Hitler and American presidents had Rome in their thoughts as they set out to fash-
ion their own powerful and durable states.

It was as a tiny city state, nestled in a circle of seven
hills on the Tiber River, not far from the Mediterranean,
that Rome began its stupendous career. In its first days,
Rome was a monarchy, with a hereditary king, but this
form of government was soon cast aside in favor of a
republic (i.e., a government without a monarch), which
was dominated by wealthy landowners known as patri-
cians. Lower-class Roman citizens, the plebeians, waged
a long struggle through which they succeeded in win-

...ting important rights for themselves. That said, great landowners and the wealthy managed to dominate Rome throughout the days of the republic and later, during the centuries of the empire.

It took hundreds of years for the Roman state to achieve dominance first in central Italy and then in the whole of the Italian peninsula. The Romans conquered some peoples, made alliances with others, and extended Roman citizenship and lesser political rights in a patchwork across Italy as their state expanded. The great resource on which they relied for their conquests was plentiful manpower, which provided first the conscripts and later the volunteers for the fierce Roman army. The conquests netted a steady supply of slaves on which Rome depended for its agricultural labor force. By the beginning of the third century BC, Rome had become a major regional, land-based power, a republic whose government combined features of aristocratic and democratic rule — for citizens, that is, but not for slaves.

Then Rome came face to face with another power based on the southern shore of the Mediterranean, the great commercial seagoing state of Carthage. Almost accidentally, the Romans and the Carthaginians came to blows over the strategic island of Sicily, which lay between the toe of Italy and North Africa.

Before it was over, there were to be three wars fought between the foes. For a time, during the Second Punic War, as it was called, the Romans were on the very edge of defeat. Hannibal, the renowned Carthaginian general, had annihilated a Roman army at the battle of Cannae. He held all of Italy except for the walled city of Rome, to which the Romans managed to cling. Ultimately, fighting a long war of attrition, the Romans prevailed in this titanic struggle. Finally, in the third war against Carthage, Rome seized the enemy's capital and razed the city, killing almost all of its population. With victory over Carthage, Rome bestrode the western Mediterranean. It had become an empire that still had a republican form of government.[2]

When the Romans went on to defeat the Macedonians, they extended their sway into the eastern Mediterranean. As Rome's rule continued to expand, a fierce internal struggle began over what shape Rome's government would take in the future. This struggle continued for over a century in a series of violent episodes and civil wars, as the military leaders who had risen to great stature in Rome's conquests began to contest the Senate, and each other, for control of Rome itself. As a consequence of its burgeoning empire, Rome's system of government was in danger of being overturned. Military strongmen such as Sulla and Marius arose and dominated Rome for a time, reducing the Senate and other institutions to powerlessness. In the middle of the first century BC, the epic struggle reached its climax. Following the assassination of Julius Caesar, who was himself a Roman conqueror who had set out to dominate Rome,

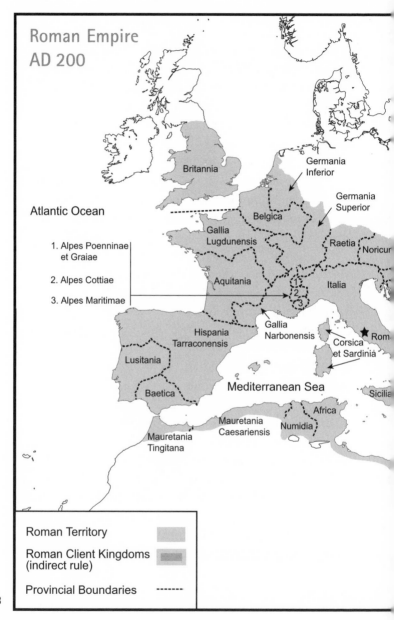

Roman Empire
AD 200

Atlantic Ocean

1. Alpes Poenninae et Graiae

2. Alpes Cottiae

3. Alpes Maritimae

Britannia

Germania Inferior

Germania Superior

Belgica

Gallia Lugdunensis

Raetia

Noricur

Aquitania

Italia

Gallia Narbonensis

Corsica et Sardinia

Rom

Hispania Tarraconensis

Lusitania

Baetica

Mediterranean Sea

Sicilia

Mauretania Caesariensis

Africa

Numidia

Mauretania Tingitana

Roman Territory	
Roman Client Kingdoms (indirect rule)	
Provincial Boundaries	-------

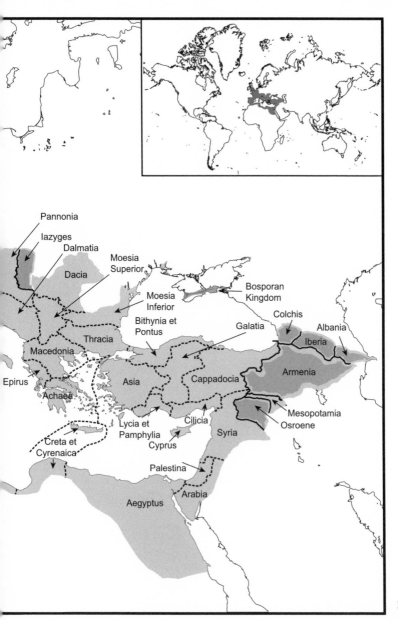

Pannonia

Iazyges

Dalmatia

Dacia

Moesia
Superior

Moesia
Inferior

Bosporan
Kingdom

Bithynia et
Pontus

Colchis

Galatia

Albania

Thracia

Iberia

Macedonia

Armenia

Epirus

Asia

Cappadocia

Achaea

Mesopotamia

Lycia et
Pamphylia

Cilicia

Osroene

Creta et
Cyrenaica

Cyprus

Syria

Palestina

Arabia

Aegyptus

there was a final civil war. The victor was Caesar's nephew Octavian, who took the name Augustus and set himself up as the first emperor of Rome.

Cleverly, Augustus Caesar disguised his transformation of the system of government by claiming that he was restoring the republic and its institutions. And though institutions such as the Roman Senate continued to exist, the emperor was the central source of governmental power. And the emperors became hereditary rulers, passing down the throne to their sons if possible.[3]

Under Augustus Caesar and his successors, Rome consolidated its rule around the whole of the Mediterranean, so that it became a Roman boast that the sea was *mare nostrum*, our sea. As has been the case with all empires, before and since Rome, the emperors had to decide which conquests were worth holding and which were not. This was a matter of determining how expensive, in treasure and in legions deployed, it would be to control a particular piece of territory. Was the territory defensible at a reasonable cost and was Roman rule in it sustainable? Would the conquest of new pieces of territory result in the capture of new supplies of slaves and of productive agricultural land that would make the enterprise worthwhile? Like other imperial rulers, Roman emperors had to deal with the problem of "imperial overstretch."

Over the centuries of the empire's existence, the Romans did decide that particular pieces of territory were not worth conquering. For instance, while the Romans conquered a large part of Britain and converted it into a Roman province, they decided against pushing their occupation north into Scotland. From their point of view, the costs outweighed the benefits. The territory was too sparse, and the inhabitants too warlike and inhospitable. The emperor Hadrian chose a solution famously used by the Chinese when they constructed the Great Wall of China to keep out invaders from the north. Hadrian's Wall was constructed across the narrow neck of land that divides England from Scotland. The barrier was intended to keep out Scottish marauders. The Romans came to a similar conclusion about most of the inhabitants of Germany and many of the inhabitants of the Arabian Peninsula. These were peoples and territories too costly to hold.

At its zenith, between the middle of the first century AD and the end of the second century AD, the Roman Empire had a population of about 120 million people. Some scholars who have studied the era have concluded that life was likely better for most people during this "golden age" than at any time prior to the eighteenth century. Golden age it may have been in some ways, but for a large percentage of the population — the slaves — life was hard and dreary. If life was difficult for most, it was very good for a few. It was an age of great landowners, whose plantations worked by slaves were productive enough to drive small farmers off the land. These Roman citizens flooded into the city, contributing to the growth of an unprecedented urban population, a population that came to depend on largesse from the rich and the state to keep them fed and entertained at the daily spectacles in the Roman Coliseum. It was this urban population that consumed the "bread and circuses" for which Rome became famous.

In addition to the great landowners, a powerful commercial class emerged during these times. These were the merchants and financiers who profited from the immense scale of economic activity in the empire. There was an enormous trade in grain, olive oil, wine, jewels and other finery, as well as in textiles and clothing. Trade proceeded along land routes, taking advantage of the roads the Romans built to the far corners of their empire. It also was carried in ships across the Mediterranean, along the Atlantic coast and across the Channel to Britain.

While the Romans never eliminated the pirates who preyed on traders, they did a better job suppressing them than any other regime until modern times. The wealthy merchants who controlled trade bore a strong resemblance to the capitalists of our own historical epoch. They earned most of their profits, however, not from their mastery over production and productive labor, but from their monopoly control of trade routes and their ability to turn a profit charging much more for a product in one place than it cost in another. Even though

Roman society remained ultimately rooted in agricultural production, cities rose across the Mediterranean world. In the cities, elites emerged that were modeled on the elites of Rome and they developed tastes and a cultural outlook much like that of the Romans, a pattern that was to be repeated in the American Empire in our day.

A great and perennially puzzling question about the Roman Empire is why Roman society progressed to a certain level of development and then advanced no further. Why did this highly complex civilization, so sophisticated in so many ways, fail to advance to a higher level of technology and economic output? By the first century AD, the Roman economic methods that were in place remained largely unchanged through the subsequent centuries of the empire's existence. Given the extent of the Roman market and the level of scientific knowledge of the time, why did Rome not undergo an industrial revolution of the kind that occurred in Europe in the eighteenth century?

Clearly, the answer to this question is not that the Romans lacked the capacity to make such a leap. Roman architecture was advanced; the Roman ability to construct stone aqueducts that brought water to cities from dozens of kilometers away has dazzled observers ever since. Indeed, a mathematician in Alexandria, in the Roman province of Egypt, even constructed a functioning toy steam engine. And it was the steam engine that was crucial to the industrial takeoff of Britain in the world's first industrial revolution.

One plausible explanation has to do with the institution of slavery. The theory is that as a consequence of the plentiful supply of cheap slave labor in the empire, there was no incentive for Roman landowners and commercial businesses to take the step toward the development of labor-saving technology, which is the idea on which the industrial revolution was based. Slavery, the engine of the empire, became the fetter of the empire as well, according to this theory.

The causes of the decline and fall of the empire have been debated ever since the Roman Empire in the west collapsed in the fifth century AD. (In the east, the empire continued, with its capital in Constantinople, for another thousand years, disappearing there only when Muslim Turks captured the city in AD 1453.)

The most famous theory about the fall of the Roman Empire was developed in Edward Gibbon's classic history of the event written in the eighteenth century.[4] Gibbon argued that the rise of Christianity in Rome, and its adoption as the official religion of the empire in the fourth century AD, ultimately doomed the empire. By sapping the energy of the Romans and directing it to the other-worldly pursuits of the Christians, the empire lost its capacity to survive, Gibbon maintained. Other theories contend that Rome fell because its upper classes refused to pay the taxation needed to keep the state sufficiently funded to sustain the Roman legions against the external pressure of Germanic invaders.

The legions themselves had fallen into disorder over a long period of time. Unable to find recruits among Roman citizens, the legions enlisted Germans, the so-called barbarians whose tribes were pressing against Rome's frontiers. And then the legions took to co-opting whole units of Germans into the Roman military. In addition, the legions in the last centuries of the empire had long since learned that they constituted the ultimate authority in Rome. Ever more frequently, legions posted on the frontier, under the command of an ambitious leader, would march back from their positions to Rome. If successful, they would overthrow the existing emperor and set up a new emperor sustained by their military power.

Whatever the explanation for the fall of the Roman Empire, what is certain is that from about the second century AD, Roman civilization failed to advance in terms of its economic techniques and its social organization. In the end, the Roman Empire decayed and was swept away. The empire that had been so central to the development of the West, and to the West's idea of what a state ought to be, collapsed, to be succeeded by centuries of decentralization and societal decay in Europe.

The Han Chinese Empire

During the first century BC, while the Romans, in the last days of the republic, were consolidating their hold on the Mediterranean, an empire that was to be the progenitor of many imperial regimes over the centuries was making its appearance in China. Both the Romans and the Chinese came to think of their regimes as rulers of the earth, and yet each was only vaguely aware of the existence of the other.

There were similarities between the Roman Empire and the Han Empire in China. Both were great agricultural civilizations, which depended ultimately on peasant labor. The difference, and it was profound, was that the Romans constructed a society based on great landowners who owned slaves, while the Chinese fashioned a powerful state that directly ruled the peasants, who were not slaves, at least not in principle. Indeed, the Han Chinese Empire came into being as a consequence of a struggle for power between an emerging central Chinese state and powerful aristocratic landowners who were much like the wealthy classes that dominated Rome. Imposing their authority over the landowners became the perennial task of Chinese imperial authorities for the next two thousand years. Sometimes they were successful in that task, while at other times the landowners rose up and defied the central government. During such periods, China became a land of feuding warlords and disparate regions.

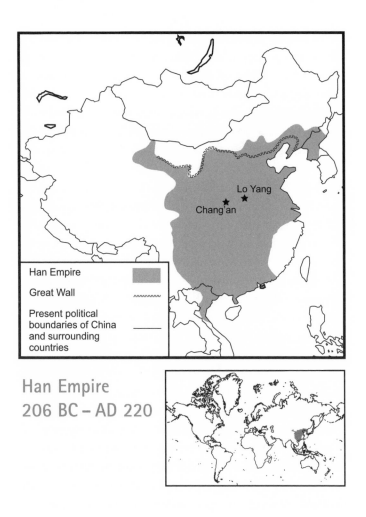

Han Empire
206 BC – AD 220

While Rome was an empire in which a powerful landowning class was a pillar of the empire, in China those who controlled the state pushed the aristocrats to one side and set up their own pyramid of power. The state taxed the peasants, taking a portion of the food they produced. That payment funded the Chinese state. From the foodstuffs that were amassed and sold for money, the whole bureaucracy of the Chinese state was financed, from the emperor at the top to the local tax collector. And taxes paid for the raising and sustaining of the Chinese army and for defense works, such as the Great Wall of China, erected against outside invaders. Under the imperial government, the path to power involved climbing up the steps of the state hierarchy, which in principle was open to all citizens. Wealth and prestige, rather than the accumulation of ownership of large amounts of land, were the ample rewards for a successful career, although property ownership was always a temptation.[5]

By knitting together the immense territory and population of China, a powerful empire was established. By itself, China had a population that rivaled that of Europe. During the historical periods when the central authority in China succeeded in extending its sway over the whole of China, its accomplishment was the equivalent of creating one government for all of Europe — something even the Romans never managed. With the power it acquired by uniting China, the Chinese state amassed the military capacity to extend its authority into the territory of neighboring peoples. The empire pushed into the Korean peninsula, into Southeast Asia and into Tibet.

At various times in Chinese history, the empire was unable to sustain itself against the invasion of its territory by the Mongol peoples to the north. Great Mongol empires rose and fell, propelled by the military prowess of the horse-riding peoples of the steppes, who succeeded at times in extending their power all the way from China to eastern Europe. The empires of the peoples of the steppes, such as that of Genghis Khan, did not last long. Launched by one dominant leader, the next generation of leaders, often the sons of the founder, fell out, fought each other and the empire broke into smaller parts.

In the case of China, while the Mongols established their power at various times, over time the Chinese succeeded in assimilating the invaders, who then reverted to trying to run China according to the same principles used by earlier Chinese regimes. Despite the differences between them, it is reasonable to include the Roman and the Han Chinese empires under the broad heading of slave or peasant empires — that is, empires in which a small class of rulers derived their wealth from an enormous peasantry.

The Spanish Empire

The next type of empire to emerge was the mercantile empire. The Spanish Empire, which rose to become a world power, fits into this category. It served as the example for both the French and British empires that followed in its path. The Spanish Empire came to embody all of the passion, energy, religiosity and rapacity of the Europe of its time, during the transition from the Middle Ages (twelfth to fourteenth century AD) to early capitalism (fifteenth to seventeenth century AD).

The empire was mounted on the rather slender base of two Spanish kingdoms, Castile and Aragon, which were bound together as a consequence of the marriage in 1469 of Princess Isabella of Castile and Prince Ferdinand of Aragon. Much the larger of the two kingdoms was Castile, with its capital in Madrid, while the capital of Aragon was in Barcelona. Late fifteenth-century Spain was still embroiled in the long-term struggle between its Christian kingdoms and the Muslim power established in the south. That struggle ended in 1492 with the defeat of the Muslim regime in Granada by the armies of Isabella and Ferdinand, who had both by then assumed the crowns in their respective kingdoms. It was the same year that Christopher Columbus undertook his historic voyage across the Atlantic in the pay of the two monarchs. These twin events, the unification of Spain under Isabella and Ferdinand, and Spain's encounter with the Americas, opened the way for the creation of a Spanish Empire.

No less important had been the development in the preceding decades in both Spain and Portugal of new kinds of ships, the caravels and the galleons, which were superior to earlier types of vessels, in being able to undertake lengthy ocean voyages.

For the Spaniards, the Americas were reached in an effort to find an oceanic route to Asia. Columbus and other explorers of the day knew that the world was round and calculated that if they traveled west far enough they would reach the eastern shores of Asia. The chief underlying motive for such expeditions was the hope for profits that would be made in establishing trade between Europe and Asia. There was a huge appetite among the upper classes in Europe for Asian spices, especially pepper, and for Asian silks. Soon enough, the Spaniards understood that they had discovered a continent that lay between Europe and Asia and they quickly learned that the Americas held bounties of their own that could make them rich. The immediately available wealth in the Americas was held by the indigenous civilizations that had established their own empires — the Aztecs, the Maya and the Incas.[6]

The so-called Conquistadores, who led expeditions to pry loose the wealth of these empires, were financed in Europe by bankers and investors from many parts of the continent. In addition to Spanish investors, there was money from Genoa, Germany, France, Holland and Britain. These ventures were undertaken not by the

Spanish Empire 1784

Viceroyalty of
New Spain

Viceroyalty of
New Granada

Viceroyalty
of Peru

Viceroyalty of
Rio de la Plata

Spain

Mad

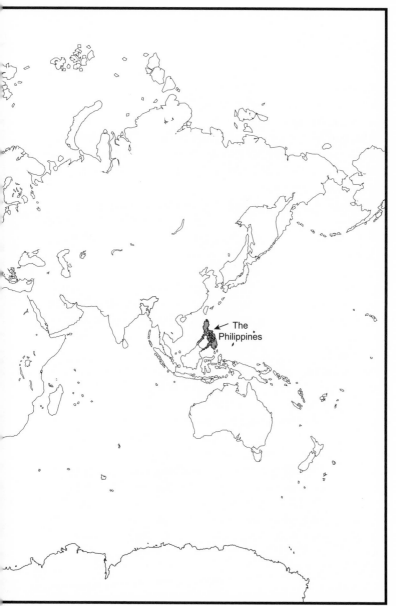

The
Philippines

Indigenous American Civilizations

Three indigenous civilizations that rose and fell in the Western Hemisphere were those of the Maya, the Incas and the Aztecs. The empires of the Aztecs and the Incas were destroyed by invading Spaniards in the sixteenth century.

The first of the three civilizations to emerge was that of the Maya, whose homeland was in the Yucatan in southern Mexico, Guatemala, northern Belize and western Honduras. Mayan civilization originated in the Yucatan as early as 2600 BC. Between AD 200 and 900, the classic period in the history of the Maya, a large number of independent states ruled by nobles and kings existed side by side. No single kingdom ever emerged to dominate the Maya and establish an empire.

Engaged in intensive agriculture on land cleared of forest, the Maya constructed cities whose centers featured temple-pyramids, monuments and palaces. Extensive trade routes were established by the Maya, who were skilled potters and weavers. Around AD 900, as a consequence of ecological disaster brought on by overpopulation, drought and the exhaustion of the land they farmed, the southern Mayan kingdoms collapsed. While the northern Mayan kingdoms continued until AD 1200, they too collapsed for similar reasons.

The second of the indigenous civilizations was that of the Incas. Beginning in the early fifteenth century, the Inca tribe extended its rule over an enormous portion of South America, eventually extending from the southern reaches of contemporary Colombia to central Chile. Inland the empire stretched across the Andes Mountains into the great Amazon forest. The empire was structured so as to superimpose an Incan elite over local elites that remained in place. This feature, despite the enormous difference in the technologies of the two systems, is similar to the structure of the American Empire, in which an American elite and global system operate through states that have their own elites.

At the time of the intrusion of the Spaniards into Incan territory, the empire was itself divided as a result of a conflict between two claimants for the title of supreme Inca. One claimant held power in the south, in the Incan capital of Cusco, while the other claimant had his power base in the north, in the city of Cajamarca.

The Aztec civilization, which emerged in the vicinity of Mexico City, reached its pinnacle between the fourteenth and the early sixteenth centuries AD. Among the Aztecs, one of the tribes of the Mexica, the Tenochca, emerged from a long period of struggle as the dominant force. The Tenochcas established the great island city of Tenochtitlan, with its temples, roads, an aqueduct system and a causeway connecting the city to the mainland. The ruins of Tenochtitlan lie beneath contemporary Mexico City.

In the crowded human landscape of central Mexico, the Aztec Empire, also known as the triple alliance, was adept not only at defeating its foes militarily but at sustaining itself by building alliances and spreading its cultural power. Since Aztec armies were not vastly superior to those of their enemies, ideological and cultural strategies were deployed to keep the empire on top. At annual festivities, Aztec rulers, in the presence of invited leaders from vassal cities and even chiefs from the cities of potential adversaries, advertised their military might and showed off their wealth and fine jewels. It was all done to overawe those they dominated, much in the manner of the visit of a foreign leader to the White House today. The export of culture and values, as well as conspicuous displays of arms and wealth, have been key to American success as they were to the success of the Aztecs.

Spanish state but by the private enterprise of the day. Rather than exploration, the goal was profit.

Early in the sixteenth century, Hernando Cortés led one such expedition into the heart of Aztec territory in central Mexico. With his small force, making use of an alliance with enemies of the Aztecs, and deploying horses and primitive guns unknown to the indigenous population, Cortés eventually managed to seize control of the territory and to overturn the Aztec Empire. In a similar expedition, launched from the west coast of South America, Fernando Pizarro achieved a victory over the Incas. One result of these conquests was that the Spaniards plundered a vast quantity of gold and silver. When their ships returned to Spain laden with bullion, all Europe was soon abuzz with the fabulous riches to be won in the New World.

It was not long before the Spaniards turned from mere plunder to more systematic ways to extract wealth from the New World. Indigenous people were forced to work in gold, and more often, in silver mines. When local labor proved insufficient, the Spaniards established a large-scale slave trade, transporting slaves from Africa to their mines and plantations in the Americas.

Wealth extracted from Spain's rising empire transformed the balance of power in Europe. Investors and financiers grew rich as a result of the gold and silver netted by their investments. Spain, with its new wealth, became an important importer of products from other parts of Europe. The Spanish state, which took a share of the bounty in the form of royalties, found the means to vastly expand its armies. Soldiers from across Europe flocked to join the Spanish army. Spanish forces were involved in wars in many parts of Europe, especially in the eighty-year-long war from the mid-sixteenth century to the mid-seventeenth century in which the people of the Netherlands fought and freed themselves from Spanish domination.

The Spaniards not only extended their power in Europe, they established a foothold in Asia, with the Philippines as their central base. From Manila, the Spaniards set up a trade network that brought Chinese and Japanese goods to European markets, often via a trans-Pacific shipping route that transferred goods first to Mexico and from there to Europe. With its role in Asia, the Americas and Europe, the Spaniards created what some scholars regard as the first global empire.

The British and French Empires

The lessons of the Spanish Empire were not lost on other Europeans, who quickly sought ways to follow in their footsteps. In sixteenth-century England, bursting with the energies of the Elizabethan Age, companies were established to discover new trading routes — initially as in the case of the Spaniards, with the goal of reaching Asia. The British tried sailing to Asia via northern routes so that they would not directly come into conflict with the

Spaniards and the Portuguese who monopolized the southern routes. British expeditions sought first a Northeast and then a Northwest Passage to Asia. The Northeast ventures did not lead to a shipping route to the Orient, but they did take English ships to Archangel on the frigid coast of northern Russia. A flourishing trade link with Russia was the result. The quest for the Northwest Passage continued for longer — indeed, it has been revived in our own era, with American efforts to ship Alaskan oil to eastern American markets by sailing through the Arctic waters of northern Canada. As a consequence of climate change, the permanent ice cover that hampered shipping in the past is fast disappearing. Over the next couple of decades, the Northwest Passage could become a major shipping route for petroleum and other products and a zone of sovereignty disputes.

The English also directly challenged the Spaniards on the seas on the routes that were vital to their own empire. Henry Morgan set himself up as a pirate whose vocation was to raid and capture Spanish ships to rob them of their gold and silver. To us that may not seem to be a respectable occupation, but investors in England were happy to put up capital to finance such missions and the English monarchy did not stand in the way of so-called privateers who were, in fact, pirates.

John Hawkins, who hailed from a seagoing family in the west of England, found another way to cash in on the profits of the Spanish Empire. With capital to finance him from British merchants, he led expeditions to Guinea in West Africa to capture and purchase men and women there. His men attacked villages, burning crops and shelters and seizing victims. Sometimes, when the villagers had been warned of an impending attack, they fought back and killed and wounded members of Hawkins' force.

The captured Africans were herded into the miserable holds of the English ships, where they were held with little food and water during the long transatlantic voyage, and often for weeks more as the ships went from port to port in the Caribbean seeking to sell the slaves to the Spaniards. This was often a perilous undertaking because it was a violation of Spanish law for merchants in the Spanish New World to purchase slaves from anyone other than Spanish suppliers of this human cargo. Using force and the threat of force, the English were often able to cajole the Spaniards into buying the slaves.

While these early English ventures created only a minor nuisance for the Spanish Empire, the challenges became more significant as time passed. In 1588, under the command of Francis Drake, the English defeated the Spanish Armada in an historic sea battle off the south coast of England. Not only was the Spanish mission to subdue England halted, the English took the first step toward making themselves the masters of the sea, the ultimate underpinning of the British Empire in the coming centuries.[7]

Gold and silver were much in the minds of the English and the French as they took to the seas in search of treasure in the late sixteenth and early seventeenth centuries. While the eastern coast of North America was by then relatively well known, the absence of obvious treasures there made the continent seem uninviting in contrast to what the Spaniards had found further south. But treasures of a different sort soon made their attractions felt. When John Cabot sailed across the North Atlantic in the late 1490s, he noticed the immense supply of codfish off the coast of Newfoundland, pools of fish so thick that a sailor could scoop them up with a net. Within a century of his discovery, fishing vessels from England, France and other countries were making a fortune from the cod fishery, feeding an enormous European population with their catch.

Onshore, the newcomers also found native populations willing to sell them furs, for which there was a large demand in Europe for the manufacture of men's hats. When Samuel de Champlain signed on as a mapmaker and geographer for the first French expedition to establish a settlement in 1604, his job was to look out for places from which mineral treasures might be extracted. To the south, a few years later, the English began establishing settler colonies, some motivated by the desire of colonists for religious freedom, others motivated by commerce driven by demand for new crops such as tobacco.

By the eighteenth century, the British (England and Scotland were united in 1707) and the French empires had become the great competitors of the age. The glory days of the Spanish Empire were in the past. Much of the treasure from the Spanish Empire had ended up in the hands of merchants and financiers in other European countries. Gold and silver had done as much harm as good to Spain's own economy, driving up the price of goods there, which priced Spanish producers out of other markets. Spain's imports vastly exceeded its exports, a problem that plagues the Americans today. Finally, by the eighteenth century, British and French military prowess had outstripped that of the Spaniards.

The early British Empire was also a mercantile undertaking, a search for profits, with ventures paid for by British investors in many parts of the world. Monopoly ventures licensed by the crown included the Muscovy Company, which traded with Russia through Archangel; the East India Company, which ended up ruling much of India from the mid-eighteenth to the mid-nineteenth century; and the Hudson Bay Company, which ran a fur-trading empire in North America, until its vast territory was taken over by Canada in 1870. In the British Empire, the theory of mercantile economics was applied. Colonies were established to make profits for the mother country. In the colonies, settlers were not supposed to engage in manufacturing that would compete with producers in Britain itself. And trade to and from the colonies was supposed to be carried out in British and colonial ships, with foreign ships not allowed to participate. In many cases, these rules were broken by colonists who found it in their interest to trade with other countries. For instance, a thriving trade was carried out between New Englanders and Acadians before Acadie (Nova Scotia) was annexed by Britain under the Treaty of Utrecht in 1713.

One part of the British Empire developed so quickly that it took on characteristics of a metropolitan power, with its own banks, merchants and even manufacturing. By the mid-eighteenth century, the thirteen colonies were outgrowing the limitations placed on them by the British imperial system. The consequence was the American Revolution, 1776-1783, which resulted in independence for the United States of America. The First British Empire had been shattered. But a new and ultimately larger Second British Empire was in the making.

The Second British Empire

The key to the Second British Empire was the Industrial Revolution, which was completed by Britain between about 1780 and 1830. Over the course of this half century, Britain became the "workshop of the world," the first industrialized country on the planet. Even though British industry was rudimentary by later standards, the British enjoyed a major advantage over other producers in the world's markets, particularly in the textile industry. There is much truth in the contention that the British Empire was based on cotton.

By the 1830s and 1840s, the consequences of the Industrial Revolution for Britain's position in the world led British elites to rethink the country's economic policies and to adopt an outlook at odds with the ideas underpinning the rules of mercantilism. Since the British were the most efficient producers of goods in the world, they saw little sense in insisting on restricting trade to their own empire. Why not sell to everyone and buy raw materials and food from the cheapest possible sources? The result was that Britain dismantled the mercantilist regulations and took up the cause of free trade. In an economic sense, they were making the whole world their empire, not just the parts of it where the Union Jack flew.

During this period, British writers proclaimed that free trade was good for everyone, that it would make both buyers and sellers more prosperous, and that it would promote a more peaceful world by making nations economically dependent on one another. Since that day, it has been commonplace for economic thinkers in countries that have the most efficient industry — first Britain, then the US, followed by Japan and now China — to believe that free trade is inherently virtuous, and to dismiss those who oppose free trade as backward protectionists.

Within a few decades, the British faced severe chal-

British Empire

London

Great
Britain

British Territory, 1860

Territory acquired by 1914

Territory acquired by 1918

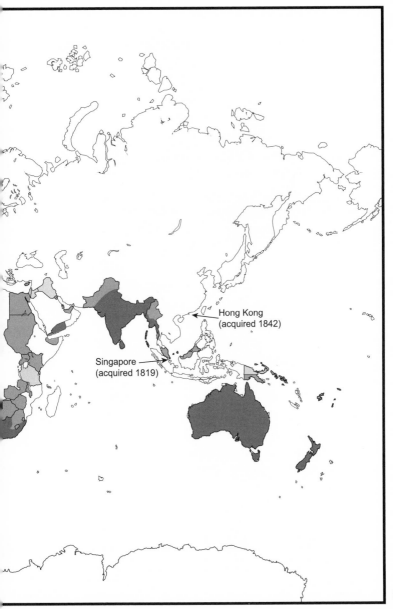

Hong Kong
(acquired 1842)

Singapore
(acquired 1819)

lenges to their economic supremacy from the Germans, the Americans, the French and later the Japanese. As these challenges mounted, the prevailing opinion among Britain's ruling elites was that the formal empire was worth keeping, that there were benefits to holding onto colonies where Britain enjoyed definite advantages over its competitors. For instance, in India, by far the most populous country in the empire, British banks, manufacturers and railway companies kept their special privileges in defiance of the theory of free trade.

The British Empire became the first and leading case of the third type of empire, the capitalist empire. As the first industrialized country in the world, Britain also became financially dominant globally. British financiers and investors had plenty of capital to invest in other parts of the world, much of the capital going to places in the empire such as Canada, where the British invested heavily in building railways. Other investments flowed to the United States, the largest single recipient of British investment, and to South America, which became a virtual British economic colony, even though very little of the continent was actually under British rule.

The Bank of England, Britain's central bank, became the world's key central banker, the way the US Federal Reserve is today. Nicknamed the "Old Lady of Threadneedle Street" (its address in London) the bank set interest rates for most of the world and thereby decided whether capital would be easy or difficult for foreigners to obtain. The Bank of England had a major influence on development projects everywhere in the world.

Britain's world position depended on its central role as global financier. It also depended on the prowess of the Royal Navy. During the eighteenth and early nineteenth centuries, the British had fought a series of wars against France, with victory finally obtained over Napoleon at the Battle of Waterloo in 1815. After Waterloo, Britain's position as master of the seas was assured, and the number of men and ships needed by the Royal Navy declined dramatically.

Just as the United States is determined, as a matter of policy, to maintain its military superiority in comparison to all other countries, the British were intent on keeping the Royal Navy supreme. British governments decided on what became known as the "two navy" standard, the idea being that the Royal Navy must remain equivalent in power at least to the next two largest navies combined.

Remarkably, Britain managed to retain its control of the seas, and therefore of the highways to the diverse parts of its empire, without spending an enormous amount on defense. Defeating France in the earlier wars had cost Britain huge amounts of money, and had driven the British government into debt. But after Waterloo, the debts were paid off, taxes fell and Britain managed to avoid the problem of costly "imperial overstretch" for many decades.

Challenges to the British Empire

In the last years of the nineteenth century, Britain's easy lead over potential challengers came to an end. The United States became the world's leading industrial power, with the world's largest national market. Closer to home, and militarily much more threatening, Germany developed into a great industrial power, surpassing Britain's industrial production. In that era economic and military might were measured in terms of a country's annual production of steel and coal and its available manpower for military service. By contrast, today military might is measured in terms of a country's overall economic output, but critically as well, in terms of its technological prowess and the size of its defense budget.

In the same decades as Britain faced economic challenges, the great powers of Europe set out to seize whatever colonial territory they could still obtain. France, Germany, Italy, the Netherlands and Belgium were all following in the path of the British in their drive to establish their own empires. And even though the Americans did not use the term "empire," they were consolidating their dominance in the Western Hemisphere. As a result of the Spanish-American War in 1898, the US ended up in possession of Puerto Rico and the Philippines. Japan, determined to avoid falling under the control of the Western powers, pushed ahead with its own program of rapid industrialization. By the end of the nineteenth century, Japan was ready to take on the other powers in East Asia. In 1895, the Japanese seized Korea and Formosa. In 1905, Japan defeated Russia in the Russo-Japanese War, a quarrel over the eastern reaches of Asia, and demonstrated to the world that a new imperial power had arrived on the scene.

During the first decade of the twentieth century, the great powers of Europe were divided into two opposing military blocs, with Britain drawn to the side of France and Russia against Germany, Austria-Hungary and Italy. (Italy ended up on the other side when she entered World War I in 1915.) From a British standpoint, the most potent challenger was Germany, which not only had surpassed Britain as an industrial power, but was straining to build a world-class navy that could challenge the supremacy of the British at sea. When World War I broke out in 1914, it could be said to have many causes, but the ultimate goal of the contenders was to establish mastery in Europe. The war, however, not only ended the global dominance of the British Empire, it ended Europe's claim to be the center of global power. Entering the war in 1917, the United States lent decisive aid to the Anglo-French war effort, dooming Germany to defeat.[8]

It would take another world war for the struggle for mastery to have a clear result. In 1945, the United States and the Soviet Union emerged from the Second World War as superpowers. From our vantage point, that date also signaled the beginning of American dominance of the global system.

Adolf Hitler's Third Reich

The short-lived, genocidal empire of Adolf Hitler was thrust upon the world on January 30, 1933, when the coterie of advisers around President Paul von Hindenburg convinced the aged head of state to call on the leader of the National Socialist German Workers' (Nazi) Party to assume the position of chancellor. In the years following Germany's devastating defeat in the First World War and the harsh Treaty of Versailles imposed on the country in June 1919 by the victorious allied powers, Hitler's Nazis were among the movements that rose up to seek revenge. The Nazis, who despised democracy, believed in a society in which one man, their leader, would be the voice of the German nation, and that supreme power would rest with him. In their drive to avenge Germany's defeat, they cloaked themselves in the theory that Germans and other Aryans were racially superior, and that they had the right to rule other lesser peoples. Above all, they preached hate against the Jews, who constituted a tiny percentage of Germany's population, accusing them of fostering all the country's ills.

Hitler had vowed in his book *Mein Kampf*, written in the early 1920s, that he would rid Germany of the Jews and that he would rearm the country. He foresaw a drive to the east, in which Nazi armies would conquer central Europe and the Soviet Union and create "living space" for the so-called German master race. While Hitler's armed thugs remained a marginal political force during the 1920s, with the onset of the Great Depression in 1929 the movement attracted increasing numbers of Germans, especially those in the middle classes and in rural areas. Critical to their rise and growing electoral success was adherence to the cause of major industrialists and bankers who came to see Hitler as a barrier against communism. American industrialist Henry Ford, a virulent anti-Semite who had published newspapers and books alleging a Jewish conspiracy to rule the world, was an inspiration to the Nazis.

Once in office, Hitler acquired control over the army, police and communications in Germany. He turned his own brown-shirted storm troopers loose on his political opponents, and in an atmosphere of terror, he won elections that gave him control of the German Reichstag (parliament). Hitler pushed an Enabling Act through the Reichstag that served as the legal basis for his dictatorship. Within a few months, the Nazi Party became the only legal political party. Free trade unions were abolished, newspapers critical of the regime were banned, and books contrary to the ideas of the Nazis were burned. By the summer of 1934, Hitler had erected a totalitarian dictatorship, in which resistance to his rule was punishable by death. Jews lost their German citizenship, were driven out of the professions and were quickly reduced to misery. Thousands of people were incarcerated in concentration camps that sprang up around Germany.

The governments of Britain and France, also concerned by what they saw as the threat of the Soviet Union and communism, attempted to appease Hitler. They stood by as his troops reoccupied the Rhineland in 1936 and as his legions marched into Austria in 1938. In September 1938, the British and French agreed at a conference with Hitler and Benito Mussolini, the fascist dictator of Italy, to hand over the Sudetenland, a frontier region of Czechoslovakia in which Germans constituted the majority of the population. In March 1939, Hitler occupied the rest of the Czech lands. Increasingly resistant to Hitler's aggressive moves, the British and French tried to prevent the Germans from invading Poland. They sought a military alliance with the Soviet Union. In August 1939, however, Hitler made a deal with Soviet leader Joseph Stalin. Under the pact, Hitler would be allowed to invade and occupy western Poland and the Soviet Union would invade the eastern region of the country.

On September 1, 1939, Hitler's armies smashed their way into Poland, and a few days later Britain, France, Canada and other British Empire countries declared war on Germany. In the spring of 1940, the Nazis invaded Western Europe, quickly overwhelming Norway, Denmark, Holland, Belgium and then France. The French surrender was followed by an assault by the German Air Force on Britain in the summer of 1940, in which the Royal Air Force managed to hold its own against the Germans. On June 22, 1941, Hitler launched the military assault on the Soviet Union that had been his obsession from the early days of his career.

At first, the invasion of the Soviet Union went well for the Nazis. Their armies quickly reached the gates of Leningrad and then Moscow. The German occupiers set up a cruel regime, plundering the countryside and reducing the inhabitants to misery and starvation. In December 1941, however, the strategic position of Nazi Germany was altered drastically. On December 6, the Soviets launched a counterattack at Moscow and threw the German armies back. The next day, the Japanese attacked Pearl Harbor. A few days later, Hitler declared war on the United States. Although the Germans resumed the offensive in 1942, taking their armies into Stalingrad and almost to the Caspian Sea, Germany was now at war with the Soviet Union, the British Empire and the United States.

The German invasion of eastern Europe brought millions of Jews within their net. Death camps, such as those at Auschwitz and Treblinka, were established and Hitler and his top lieutenants launched what they called the Final Solution, the deliberate murder of all the Jews of Europe. By the end of the war, six million Jews had died in the Holocaust. In addition to the Jews, the Nazis murdered Gypsies, the disabled and homosexuals, and over twenty million Soviets perished during the invasion of their country.

By the summer of 1943, the Soviet armies began pushing relentlessly westward. The following spring, on June 6, 1944, the Americans, British, Canadians and Free French invaded Normandy. Attacked from the east and the west, Hitler's empire was quickly shrinking. On April 30, 1945, with Russian soldiers only a few hundred meters away, Adolf Hitler took his own life in his bunker beneath the ruins of Berlin. Eight days later, the Germans surrendered unconditionally to the Soviets and the Western allies.[9]

Chapter 3
The American Empire

The First and Second World Wars led to the dismantling of the great European empires. In 1947, India and Pakistan became independent states, ending British dominance over what had been the heart of the British Empire. Over the next couple of decades, the rest of Britain's colonies in Asia, Africa and the Caribbean achieved self-government. The French fought and lost bloody wars against movements for national liberation in Vietnam and Algeria and their imperial system went the way of the British. The Belgian, Dutch and Portuguese imperial holdings were similarly lost. From the vantage point of the 1960s, it seemed reasonable to conclude that the age of empire was at an end.[1]

What observers at the time often failed to recognize was that the Soviet and American states presided over empires — the Soviet Empire an old-fashioned affair whose demise we have already discussed. The American Empire, however, was something new. For many decades, it was not widely seen as an empire. Even today, while many scholars and analysts, including Americans, use the word "empire" to describe America's place in the global system of power, the term remains highly controversial in mainstream political discourse in the United States.

Everyone agrees that the United States is the world's most powerful state, that it is now the world's only superpower. And scholars widely agree that it is proper to call the United States a "hegemonic" power, that is, a power that exercises long-term domination over other states in the global system. The controversy concerns the claim that the United States today is at the center of a global empire.[2]

It is easy to see why many Americans, including American political leaders, reject the use of the word empire to describe American global power. While the Europeans were proud to think of themselves as running empires, the United States established itself as an independent state as a result of a revolutionary war against the British Empire. The American Revolution was the first anti-imperialist war of modern times. The proud legacy of the revolution makes it invidious for Americans to accept the idea that their country has evolved into an imperial power, indeed that it has become the greatest imperial power in history. In fact, in our age the concept of empire is widely rejected, at least rhetorically, by political leaders in virtually all parts of the world.

Why then do friends and foes alike of the United

States now contend that there is an American Empire? The claim that there is an American Empire turns on the fact that the United States exercises long-term, decisive power within the global system and has a determining influence on the social, political, military and even cultural outcomes in a very large number of countries around the world. As we have seen, important parts of the British Empire were not formally British territory. The fact, therefore, that the United States has not annexed foreign territory does not negate the claim that there is a vast informal American Empire.

Pillars of the American Empire

The American Empire is a new type of empire, with some characteristics in common with the capitalist empires of the European powers in the nineteenth and twentieth centuries. But the American Empire displays features that differentiate it from all previous empires. First, let us review the extent of American power in the global system, which can be said to rest on four pillars — economic, military, political and cultural.

The United States has been the world's leading economic power for well over a century. It not only has the largest economic output of any country, but it has enjoyed technological leadership in key fields for an extended period of time. American economic domination of the world reached its peak at the end of the Second World War, in 1945, when the United States produced half of the goods and services in the world. This unusual level of supremacy was achieved, of course, because its major competitors had had their economies largely destroyed as a result of the war. Since the end of the war, American global economic power has declined dramatically in relative terms. That is to say that while the American economy is much larger than it was then, the world economy has grown much more rapidly over the same period than the American economy. Today, the United States produces about 20 percent of the world's goods and services, still a very substantial proportion. (When discussing American global economic decline, it is important to point out that this decline is relative, not absolute.) And while the United States still has the highest Gross Domestic Product (total output of goods and services) of any country in the world, its GDP is now second to that of the European Union, with its 25 member countries. With the rapid rise of the economic output of China, India and other major countries such as Brazil, it is reasonable to project that the US share of global economic output will decline further, likely to about 15 percent of the world total over the next decade or two.

Military power is the second pillar on which US supremacy rests. No country has ever dominated the world militarily to the extent that the United States now does. The United States currently spends over $500 billion a year on its military, which is as much as the expenditure of the next sixteen countries combined. In fact, US military spending is nearly as much as the military spending of all the other countries in the world combined. When Britain was supreme in the world in the nineteenth century, its military spending was not nearly as high as US spending is today as a proportion of the global total. As noted earlier, the British made it their policy to keep their navy at least as large as the navies of the next two powers combined. The current policy of the United States government is to maintain American military supremacy into the indefinite future.

In September 2002, the administration of President George W. Bush published a military blueprint for the future stating that it was US policy to ensure that no other power would be able to challenge the military supremacy of the United States. The policy of the Bush administration, and of earlier administrations, has been to prevent any military challengers from emerging. Military strength has always been one of the requisite requirements of empire and the United States government, well aware that it cannot dominate the world economically over the long term, is determined that the military pillar will be sustained.

A symbol of that determination is that in the aftermath of the terror attacks on New York City and Washington, DC on September 11, 2001, the Bush administration claimed the right, in clear violation of international law, to carry out pre-emptive military strikes against countries that the US government believed were preparing to attack the United States. The US invasion of Iraq in March 2003, in conjunction with a number of other countries, but without the support of the United Nations Security Council, was justified as a pre-emptive attack against a regime that was developing weapons of mass destruction to attack the United States. Subsequently, it has been proven that the claim that Iraq possessed such weapons was based on faulty intelligence. The charge that the Bush administration, having decided to invade Iraq, pressured the Central Intelligence Agency and other agencies to provide reports validating the claim that Saddam Hussein's regime was developing chemical and nuclear weapons, has become a contentious issue in American politics.

US military supremacy is sustained by the positioning of US forces in bases in dozens of countries located on every continent. The country's nuclear arsenal is second to none, and it is the policy of the current US administration to continue developing new kinds of nuclear weapons and not to sign on to the nuclear weapons test ban treaty. The US government also refuses to commit to the anti-land mines treaty, which has been signed by most countries in the world. Under the current administration, the US revoked its commitment to the anti-missile defense treaty signed by the United States and the Soviet Union in 1972. The policy of the Bush administration is to develop an anti-missile defense shield to protect the United States against a potential nuclear missile attack.

The third pillar of US global power — the political pillar — rests on the power the US exerts in direct negotiations with other countries, through its membership in regional groupings of countries such as the Organization of American States and through its enormous power in international economic bodies such as the World Trade Organization, the International Monetary Fund and the World Bank. This form of power, often described as "soft power," is distinguished from the direct coercion involved in the use of military or "hard power."[3] In all of these forums, the US has used its enormous influence to pressure other countries to adopt the form of capitalism it prefers, a system in which government regulation is minimal and maximum room is left for corporations, foreign as well as domestic, to do as they please. The decisive position occupied by the United States in the International Monetary Fund, for example, has often been used to pressure countries that are in debt and require new loans to tide them over to drastically cut spending on health care, education and social welfare as well as to privatize publicly owned companies and open the door to investment by multinational corporations. As a consequence, social and economic policies in many Latin American countries have effectively been established in Washington, with highly negative consequences for their populations. On broad questions of trade and the right of capital to flow freely from country to country as corporations prefer, the United States has exercised crucial leverage over the policies of countries in virtually every part of the world, including Western Europe, despite the strong resistance in Europe to adopting American-style capitalism.

Cultural power is the fourth pillar of American global power. This is one of the ways in which the American Empire differs from its predecessors. While both the French and British empires were successful in exporting important elements of their cultures to elites in other countries, they were much less influential when it came to mass culture. It has been in the realm of mass culture — films, television and music — that American culture has become a truly global culture. This has had the effect of transmitting American values, products and attitudes to peoples around the world in an entirely novel way. And this has not been left to chance. Representatives of the American film and television industries, with the full support of the American state, have worked ceaselessly throughout the world since the end of the Second World War to keep the door wide open to the importation of American cultural products. These same lobbies have also exerted pressure to limit the extent to which the cultural products of other countries receive government support and are protected by government regulations to keep them viable. In English-speaking Canada, for instance, only about 2 percent of the films shown in cinemas are domestically produced, caused not least by the American stranglehold on the film distribution system in Canada. The United States government regards American cultural products as important tools in its effort to win foreigners over to the acceptance of the American view of the good life and how society should be organized.

In addition to the impact of American cultural products on people in many parts of the world, there is the crucial fact that elites in a large number of countries identify with the American global system and the way of life it promises for them and their families. Those who own businesses in Latin America or Asia whose products are fed into the production system of American multinationals — for instance in the garment industries, where low wages are the key to competitiveness — identify with the corporations they supply and with the broader arrangements of American power. Members of local elites have often been educated at American universities, where they have learned a discipline and a set of skills and have also imbibed the essentials of the American world view. In this respect, the American Empire is reminiscent of the Roman Empire, where local elites who had been molded to adopt the mores and outlook of the dominant elites in Rome played a crucial role in sustaining imperial authority.

Taken together, these four pillars of American power have sustained a role for the United States in the affairs of the world that is unique in human history. It is reasonable to conclude that the American Empire is the first truly global empire in the history of the world.

How the American Empire Works

The unique feature of the American Empire is that it operates, more than any of its predecessors, without the United States directly administering the countries that fall under its sway. This means that the US has been able to get its way in promoting what it sees as its fundamental interests without having to pay for an army of administrators, in the manner of previous empires. America has defined its fundamental economic interests as follows: the promotion of a system of relatively unregulated free enterprise that allows capital to flow freely to all parts of the world, and a system of trade that places as few barriers as possible in the way of the ability of multinational corporations to access raw materials, labor, productive facilities and markets in all parts of the world. The security interests of the United States have been defined as being closely related to these economic goals. The United States acts to prevent challengers from emerging that can threaten American military supremacy. Further, the American military is in place to ensure that the United States can protect its access to vital raw materials such as petroleum and to ensure that the US navy has free access to all the key sea passageways of the world.

Just as the Roman Empire saw it as vital to erect a

military umbrella over the world of the Mediterranean on behalf of large landowners, commercial interests and slave owners, the United States sees it as crucial to maintain military security worldwide on behalf of a global system of private capital. While the United States does not aspire to the annexation of foreign territory, it has been prepared to use force in critical areas of the world to attain the outcomes it desires on vital issues.

It should not be thought that because the American Empire is informal in its structure and relies on national governments to administer their territories, that it is a peaceful empire. From the first years of the American Republic, the United States has been involved in military action against foreign states on a regular basis. Over the course of its first century, American military expeditions were directed mainly at neighboring states, and at the territorial expansion of the American Union across the continent, where the foes were native peoples. The United States undertook an assault against the Barbary pirates, who were based in Tripoli, in North Africa, in 1805 to retaliate against the attacks made by the pirates against American shippers. In 1812, the United States declared war against Great Britain, a war provoked by the British practice of halting and searching neutral ships that were trying to reach continental European markets under the control of Britain's enemy, Napoleonic France. To get at its British foe, the Americans invaded Canada, an invasion that was successfully repulsed with no change in the frontier between the United States and British North America.

By the 1820s, the United States had come to see itself as a special power in the Americas. In 1823, the US government proclaimed the Monroe Doctrine, which has been a cornerstone of the American view of the Western Hemisphere ever since. Through the doctrine, the United States declared that it would not tolerate any new imposition of rule over peoples in the Americas by a European power. While the US did not propose to drive the British and French out of the territories they already held in the hemisphere, Washington would not tolerate any campaign on the part of Spain to retake its lost American colonies or on the part of any other European state to stake out a claim in the hemisphere. With the proclamation of the Monroe Doctrine, the United States was doing something other imperial powers have done in the past, declaring that a particular region of the world was its turf, or sphere of influence, and that other powers should stay out. The Soviet Union made such a claim to Eastern Europe following the Second World War. Japan proclaimed that East Asia was its special preserve during the 1930s and early 1940s.

Since the proclamation of the Monroe Doctrine, the United States has carried out dozens of armed interventions in the hemisphere. Among the countries subject to such occupation was Mexico, with which the US went to war in 1846 and emerged two years later with the annexation of a crescent of territory comprising the states of New Mexico, Arizona and California. In later decades, there were to be further US military interventions in Mexico. Other countries to which the US sent troops were Cuba, the Dominican Republic, Grenada, Colombia and Haiti. In the case of Panama, which the US coveted as the site for a canal to connect the Atlantic and Pacific oceans, in 1903 the US provoked a revolution in the territory, which declared its independence from Colombia, of which it had been a part. Then the US signed a long-term deal with Panama declaring the Canal Zone a special territory that would be occupied in perpetuity by US troops. In 1999, after decades of agitation on the issue in Panama, the US government relinquished full control of the canal to the government of Panama.

In 1898, the United States went to war against Spain, and during that conflict occupied Cuba and seized Puerto Rico and the Philippines. It fought a long war in the Philippines to suppress an independence movement there.

By the time the First World War broke out in 1914, the United States had made itself a regional power that had achieved dominance in the Western Hemisphere, a power that was prepared to use force in the hemisphere to protect US investors and to keep the peace in areas that were seen as vital to US interests. The great European war was to transform the global balance of

Mark Twain, Anti-imperialist

The occupation of the Philippines distressed many Americans during the first decade of the twentieth century. Renowned author Mark Twain warned that the United States was on the road to making itself an imperial power, something that was completely antithetical to the values on which the country had been founded.

"I said to myself," wrote Twain about the American intervention in the Philippines,

> here are a people who have suffered for three centuries. We can make them as free as ourselves, give them a government and country of their own, put a miniature of the American constitution afloat in the Pacific, start a brand new republic to take its place among the free nations of the world. It seemed to me a great task to which we had addressed ourselves.
>
> But I have thought some more, since then...and I have seen that we do not intend to free, but to subjugate the people of the Philippines. We have gone there to conquer, not to redeem.
>
> And so I am anti-imperialist. I am opposed to having the eagle put its talons on any other land.

power and to open the door for a much wider role for the United States. The 1914-1918 war ended Britain's century-long domination of the global system of power, bringing to a conclusion the so-called Pax Britannica (Latin for "British Peace"), the system under which

Britain dominated the world. Before the war, Britain had been the world's most important creditor power, the country with the largest amount of capital available to be lent to foreigners to undertake economic development projects. The war wiped out Britain as a great creditor power. The United States, which before the war had been a net lender, took Britain's place as the world's most important source of capital. New York replaced London as the financial capital of the world.

Militarily and politically, the United States also emerged from the conflict with enormous clout. When US President Woodrow Wilson arrived in Europe to negotiate a peace settlement in the early months of 1919, he was greeted by Europeans, foes as well as friends, with enormous hope. In the end, the Treaty of Versailles was a bitter pill for the defeated Germans to swallow. They lost territory and their armed forces were reduced from an army of millions of men during the world war to a force of 100,000 men. They were forbidden to have an air force and they had to pay an enormous sum in reparations to the victorious powers. Most odious of all, the Germans were forced to sign a war-guilt clause in which they admitted that Germany had been responsible for the war.[4]

Wilson's great achievement, along with the treaty, was to launch the League of Nations, a body that governments would join, and through which they would maintain peace among nations in the future. With the failure of the United States to ratify American membership in the League with a two-thirds vote of the US Senate, the US opted out of the new arrangement for collective security. During the 1920s and 1930s, Americans were disillusioned with the way the war had turned out. Isolation from European affairs, though not from continuing interventions in Latin America and China, became the dominant American practice during this period. The first opportunity for the United States to step forward to take the place of Britain in the world system of power had been turned down by Americans themselves.

A second opportunity soon presented itself and this time the United States assumed its new global role, from which it was not to retreat. With Britain unable to resume its former global position, Germany, Italy and Japan challenged the balance of power established following the First World War. Hitler's Nazi regime in Germany, Mussolini's fascist government in Italy and the militarist Japanese government all set out to create new empires for themselves. The Second World War broke out on September 1, 1939, with Germany's invasion of Poland, followed within a few days by declarations of war against Germany by Britain and France. The United States stayed out of the conflict until the surprise attack on Pearl Harbor, launched by Japan on December 7, 1941.

By the time the US entered the war, France had been defeated and occupied by Germany and Germany had invaded the Soviet Union. American power was instrumental in bringing about the ultimate defeat of the fascist powers in Europe and of Japan in Asia. With its use of two atomic bombs against Hiroshima and Nagasaki in the last days of the war, the United States ushered in the new and terrifying age of nuclear weapons and announced to the world that it possessed a means of destruction that no other country then had.

Even before the end of the war, in the summer of 1944, at Bretton Woods, New Hampshire, the United States and its allies made plans for how the post-war global economy was to be organized. The United States dollar, linked to gold at a price of $35 an ounce, was to be the reserve currency of the world, that is to say that all other currencies were to be convertible into US dollars at fixed rates of exchange. (Since the early 1970s when this arrangement collapsed, currencies float against one another in the marketplace, rather than having their rates of exchange fixed by agreements among governments. The US dollar still retains its position as the reserve currency of the world.)

In the years following the war, under the leadership of the US, the International Monetary Fund was set up to provide short-term loans to countries that had gone into debt and the World Bank was created to make available long-term development loans to poor countries. In 1948, the General Agreement on Tariffs and Trade, replaced in the 1990s by the World Trade Organization, was established to organize rounds of trade talks to take steps toward the ultimate achievement of free trade. As well, as part of the post-war settlement, the United Nations was established in 1945, to replace the defunct League of Nations, and to serve as a body that would promote international development and human well-being, its critical task the provision of collective security against war. The Security Council sat atop the structure of the UN, with its five permanent members the United States, the Soviet Union, the United Kingdom, France and China, each with the power to veto any resolution adopted by the Council.

In the early post-war years, as the Cold War with the Soviet Union got underway, and as it became clear that Britain could no longer shoulder the weight of its empire, the United States took up many of the positions that had previously been occupied by Britain. When Britain announced that it was withdrawing from Greece and the eastern Mediterranean, the Truman administration declared that it would take Britain's place. More importantly, the United States government announced that its policy would be to contain communism, whether communism was being promoted by external force against a country or by means of internal subversion. Under the heading of this containment policy, the United States forged military alliances around the globe and established military bases on all continents. The idea was to contain the Soviet Union and China, and in the process the United States ended up running a very large part of the world.

American Intervention

Where direct American negotiation and pressure did not result in Washington getting its way, other methods were used. In 1951, the Central Intelligence Agency sponsored a coup d'état in Iran against a nationalist government to ensure that Iranian oil would remain in the hands of a friendly regime that would do business with American petroleum companies. In 1954, when the interests of the United Fruit Company were threatened by a reform government in Guatemala, the United States sponsored a rebel force that invaded the country and threw out its government. To describe the regimes that emerged out of this type of intervention on behalf of US interests in Latin America, the term "banana republic" was coined.

In the early 1970s, the US government played a crucial role in helping prepare the way for the violent coup d'état in Chile that overturned the democratically elected government of Salvador Allende on September 11, 1973. Alarmed by the plans of the Allende government to redistribute wealth and land to workers and peasants in Chile, the Nixon administration covertly directed funds into the country to help develop the opposition to Allende. This included forging links with the Chilean military. While the CIA did not organize the coup that was carried out by General Augusto Pinochet and that led to the death of Salvador Allende and hundreds of others in the years to follow, the US was directly involved in the effort to topple Chile's socialist government.

In 1981, US President Ronald Reagan continued the US tradition of intervening in Latin America when he signed a top-secret National Security Decision Directive giving the CIA $19 million to recruit and support the Contras in Nicaragua. The Contras were right-wing armed units established to put an end to the revolution-ary Sandinista government in Nicaragua that had come to power with the overthrow of the brutal dictatorship of Anastasio Somoza Debayle in 1979. Defying a ruling by the International Court of Justice in 1986, which found the United States guilty of violating international law by using force against another state, the Reagan administra-tion continued its illegal support of the Contras by fun-neling funds to them through third parties. This was later exposed in what was called the Iran-Contra Affair.

On the mainland of Asia, the United States fought two major wars, the Korean War in the early 1950s, which halted a North Korean invasion of the south, and the Vietnam War in the 1960s and 1970s. The Vietnam War was an American catastrophe. Failing to create a successful government and society in the South in the aftermath of the French retreat from Vietnam in the 1950s, the US ultimately watched as the North Vietnamese nationalist and communist forces, in conjunction with the guerilla forces of the Viet Cong, achieved victory and the unification of the country under their rule in 1975.

The Vietnam War was a direct setback for American power in the world, not least because the American people came to revile the war and became highly suspicious of such foreign interventions that led to thousands of soldiers coming home in body bags. The war also hurt America because it coincided with the rise of serious economic competition with the United States from the Europeans and the Japanese, whose economies had recovered from the devastation of the Second World War. While the US invested heavily in developing its military prowess, the Germans and the Japanese specialized in producing products consumers in the advanced countries wanted. In the early 1970s, the United States found itself falling behind its competitors in crucial areas of industrial production, from automobiles, to television sets, to machinery. For the next two decades that competition would raise questions about whether the United States could maintain its global economic and technological lead.

During the mid-1980s, the reform process that led to the disintegration of the Soviet Empire and the Soviet Union itself by 1991 was underway. Soviet leader Mikhail Gorbachev had recognized that the West and Japan had pulled far ahead of his country in the critical area of high technology. It was his hope to modernize and reform the Soviet system. In the event, the system proved incapable of being reformed. As we have seen, the Soviet superpower slid beneath the waves in a few short years.

The collapse of the Soviet Union left the United States in an entirely unique position in the world. It became the world's only superpower. It had, however, lost the rationale that American leaders had used to build American power around the world from the time the Cold War began. That rationale had been that the United States was the crucial nation needed to build alliances to prevent the spread of communism. The collapse of the Soviet Union left American leaders in an almost visible state of embarrassment. They needed to find some new way to justify the continuance of the empire they had constructed.[5]

For a time, American leaders settled on a new concept, much used by Secretary of State Madeleine Albright during the Clinton presidency. The United States was the "indispensable nation" in the world system, she regularly repeated. These were the days when it was commonplace for people to talk of a "borderless world" and even the "end of history," the idea being that with the demise of Soviet communism all the great historical questions had been solved. It seemed that the future of the world would adhere closely to the values of American-style capitalism.

The Bush Doctrine

With the terror attacks on New York City and Washington, DC on September 11, 2001, and the subsequent US-led invasions of Afghanistan and Iraq in 2001 and 2003, a new rationale for the American role in the world developed. It came to be known as the Bush doctrine, from the ideas advanced in the addresses to Congress of President George W. Bush in the aftermath of the terror attacks, the lead-up to the invasion of Iraq and in his second Inaugural Address in January 2005. The Bush doctrine can be seen as providing no less than a rationale for the American Empire in the contemporary global setting.

At the heart of the doctrine are several overarching concepts. First, there is the notion that containment, which served during the Cold War to deter communist aggression, will not work in a world in which failed states have become havens for terrorists determined to strike out against the United States and its allies. Pre-emptive strikes against such centers are essential for the protection of the US, much the way Roman sorties against barbarians on the frontiers of the Roman Empire were necessary to protect Rome from attack. And directly linked to the idea of carrying the attack to the enemy instead of waiting for the enemy to attack America, is the idea of the "war on terrorism."

A war on terrorism is not a conventional war along the lines of a war between two states, with one side winning and the other side losing, and a peace treaty being signed. It is a war waged on one side by a great empire with the most powerful military in the world against a shadowy set of enemies who threaten the US with terror attacks along the lines of those on September 11, or even worse, and who wage an ideological struggle to mobilize large parts of the world against the US.

As critics have pointed out, a "war on terrorism" amounts to a never-ending war or permanent war. There is no clear way of measuring victory in such a war. As long as terrorism exists in any important form in any major part of the world, the war will continue. The implications of such an outlook are very important for the people of the United States, and for people in the rest of the world. In his address to the US Congress shortly after the terror attacks on September 11, 2001, President Bush stated that the countries of the world would have to decide which side they were on in the war on terrorism. If they failed to side with the United States in the conflict, they would be seen as siding with the terrorists. Not only has the United States brought immense pressure on other countries to conceive of the struggle in the same way it does, but it has worked tirelessly to oblige them to pass anti-terrorism legislation along the lines of the legislation passed in the US since September 11.

Under the US Patriot Act, passed in the months following the attacks on New York and Washington, DC, the US government has acquired a host of new powers to monitor the behavior of people in the United States and to incarcerate people for lengthy periods of time without charging them with a specific offence. Under the Patriot Act, US government agencies have broad new powers to tap phones, to eavesdrop on email correspondence, to enter libraries and bookstores and to obtain information about the books people are reading and purchasing. The Act allows the US government to hold citizens and non-citizens for long periods of time as material witnesses in ongoing investigations. In such situations, those held have no automatic right to see a lawyer and their names are not even released, making it very difficult for others to help them.

In the months following the September 11 attacks, the US government was estimated to have incarcerated well over one thousand people of Middle Eastern origin as material witnesses. When people were released from such custody, they spoke of being held in solitary confinement, often in shackles. In addition to the use of these powers at home, the US established camps in Afghanistan and at its base in Guantanamo Bay, Cuba, where it holds hundreds of men taken prisoner during the assault on Afghanistan. The men incarcerated in these camps are not recognized by the US government as enemy combatants and are therefore not accorded the rights they should enjoy under the Geneva Conventions on the holding of Prisoners of War. As a consequence, these detainees are held with no right to legal counsel, and subjected to interrogation that would not be allowed in the case of POWs. In principle, according to the US government, such detainees could be detained until the "war on terrorism" is over, which as we have seen, could be never. Critics of such methods of detention describe the camps operated by the United States as an American Gulag, naming them after the forced labor camps in the Soviet Union.

One of the reasons the United States wanted other countries to enact anti-terrorism legislation similar to the US Patriot Act was that it would allow for the establishment of close links between US authorities in the FBI, CIA and the Department of Homeland Security with authorities in other countries. Such links would assist the US in tracking terror suspects in many countries, not just in the United States. Links with countries such as Pakistan and Egypt were developed in this way. So too, links were developed with Western democracies such as Canada.

In one notorious case, in the autumn of 2002, US authorities detained a Syrian-born Canadian citizen when he arrived in New York City on a flight from Zurich. Maher Arar had planned to fly home to Ottawa from New York. Instead of deporting Arar to Canada, the US sent him first to Jordan and then to Syria, where Arar was held for ten months before being released. At home at last in Canada, Arar told the story of how he was repeatedly tortured in a Syrian prison. In response to public outrage, the Canadian government called a public inquiry to investigate how this had happened to a Canadian citizen. Testimony at the inquiry strongly implicated Canadian authorities in cooperating with their US counterparts and bearing some responsibility for what had happened. Under a Canada-US border accord, Canada had agreed to share information with the US on travelers who potentially could pose a risk to national security. It appears that Arar fell into this trap.

Under the rubric of fighting the war on terrorism, the United States and countries under American influence were creating what could be called a "surveillance state," a system in which citizens could be subjected to close scrutiny by authorities and could be held in detention without being charged with committing a crime.

The American Empire is not the first in history where the operations abroad of the empire have imperiled the liberties and democratic rights of citizens at home. While Rome was no democracy in the modern sense of the term, it enjoyed a republican system of government in which citizens had a role to play in choosing those who governed them. As we have seen, in the first century BC, at a time when Rome had imposed its rule over the whole of the Mediterranean world, struggles broke out among Roman military leaders who wanted complete power for themselves. This struggle ended with the collapse of the republic and the birth of the empire, a system enabled by the power military chieftains had gained through foreign conquests.

Similarly in Britain, while the rise of empire did not prevent the growth of democracy, it certainly retarded it. Britain's empire, from the eighteenth to the twentieth century, had the effect of prolonging the power and influence of the country's landed aristocracy. Instead of emerging as a completely post-feudal country, with industrial and financial capitalists at the helm, the empire gave the aristocracy a new lease on life. Members of aristocratic families became administrators and military officers all over the empire. In addition, the financial sector in Britain developed in response to the fact of empire.

Imperial wars against France in the eighteenth century were the crucial stimulus to the development of an advanced financial sector in the city of London. Yet instead of a close link between finance and industry, in Britain, finance and the aristocracy became tightly integrated during the period of Britain's imperial supremacy. What emerged has been called "gentlemanly capitalism," a societal form that kept a rigid class structure in place.[6] The consequence was that British industry was often short of the capital it needed to stay competitive with industrial challengers in Germany and the US. And the aristocracy kept its influence well into the twentieth century, as evidenced by the continuing power of the House of Lords and a social hierarchy based on private schools, universities geared to the upper classes, and a society in which one's accent revealed where one stood in the pecking order. Empire retarded the development of democracy in Britain, there can be no doubt.

In the United States, similar pressures exist. In American society, the general question asked is how high a price Americans should be expected to pay to export their values and social norms to other parts of the world. Less often asked is what effect its world role has on democracy in the US itself. An early warning of the dangers came in the farewell address to the nation of President Dwight D. Eisenhower in January 1961. Eisenhower alerted Americans to the problem of what he called the rise of a "military-industrial complex" in the United States. Eisenhower believed that the enormous defense-industry sector, with its close ties with the rest of American business, posed a threat to American democracy. Since that warning over four decades ago, the defense sector has grown enormously, with huge industrial clusters in many regions of the United States. American presidents, while in office, have made a concerted effort to expand defense-sector business in their home states. The links between the defense sector and American global policy are too important to be overlooked. For instance, in the aftermath of the US invasion of Iraq in March 2003, Halliburton Corporation, an engineering and defense contracting firm with close ties to the US government — Vice President Dick Cheney

Imperial Journeys

Imperial leaders have always traveled in ways that enhance their image of potency, an image designed to fill the populace with awe. Alexander the Great rode Bucephalus, a great black stallion with a white star on his forehead. Bucephalus lived to the age of thirty, dying at the end of one of Alexander's battles. The stallion was buried with full military honors. In the nineteenth century, Queen Victoria traveled in her own carriage, the royal crest emblazoned on the door, accompanied by footmen in full regalia.

What is unequalled is the splendor of the transportation arrangements of the president of the United States, who flies in one of two specially remodeled Boeing 747-200B aircraft. When the president is on board, the aircraft is known by its radio call sign, Air Force One. The aircraft is outfitted with 400 kilometers (238 miles) of electrical wiring, more than twice that found on a normal 747. The 375 square meters (4000 square feet) of floor space inside the aircraft harbors a presidential stateroom. The president also has a bedroom and a full bath. There is a presidential office, a conference/dining room, two fully equipped kitchens, a medical treatment room and secretarial offices. Up to seventy people can fly on the aircraft so that the president can transport cabinet secretaries, top aides, security personnel and favored media people. On board there are six lavatories and eighty-four telephones. The presidential jets, which can fly halfway around the world without refueling, can be refueled by military aircraft while in the air. The two aircraft, whose combined price tag was $650 million, are outfitted with an anti-missile defense system, as well as an anti-nuclear protective shield. The shield is in place to protect computers and other electronics gear, including a communications system that boasts secure voice terminals and cryptographic equipment for sending, receiving and deciphering classified messages.

A C-5 Galaxy heavy transport aircraft flies to the destination in advance of Air Force One. The cargo plane delivers the president's bullet-proof limousine, a standby limousine, a fully equipped ambulance, and in some cases, an armored helicopter called Marine One. The limousine, Cadillac One, is a specially designed and equipped version of the Cadillac deVille, whose exact dimensions are a state secret. The automobile's thirteen-centimeter (five-inch) thick armor is able to withstand an attack by rocket-propelled grenades. The vehicle, which has an armor-plated underside, is able to keep passengers safe in the event of a biological or chemical attack.

When the president lands at the airport in a foreign country, his advance security team has already been long on the ground, informing the locals about what will and will not be tolerated. For instance, in London, one of only fifteen cities outside the US where there is a permanent US Secret Service Office, a presidential visit is planned by American operatives who have an intimate knowledge of the setting. As soon as a visit is announced, the Secret Service team begins its muscular negotiations with local authorities, deciding which sites the president will visit and laying down requirements for his protection. No other leaders' functionaries are allowed to take such an active part in laying on security on foreign soil. A trip abroad by President George W. Bush, such as the president's visit to England in November 2003, and to Afghanistan, India and Pakistan in the winter of 2006, is classified in the US as a "national special security event."

was its former Chief Executive Officer — has received contracts for work in Iraq worth billions of dollars. While US taxpayers are paying in excess of $80 billion a year to fund US operations in Iraq, for Halliburton and similar companies, the occupation of Iraq has been a gigantic moneymaker.

The influence of special interests within American business, defense-sector industries and petroleum companies has raised serious concerns in the United States. Today American politics, particularly at the presidential level, has become an extremely costly affair. Hundreds of millions of dollars are spent on presidential campaigns, so much money that in the 2004 election, both the Republican and Democratic candidates turned down matching funds from the federal government that would have limited their permissible spending. The undue influence of corporations with a huge stake in the outcome of elections is well documented. The consequence is that American democracy is now remote from the ideals that motivated it in the past. The idea of a government close to the people whose conduct can be affected by ordinary Americans who can enter the political process is an ideal that may still find favor at July 4 celebrations. Increasingly, it has little to do with the reality of contemporary America. As in the case of Britain, empire and the defense of the empire have cast a shadow across American democracy.

Chapter 4
Cracks in the American Imperial Armor

All empires face challenges, both external and internal. It is extremely costly for a society to acquire an empire and it remains costly, once the empire has been established, to sustain it. As we have seen, empires are subject to "imperial overstretch," the problem of deciding how large the empire should be, what is defensible and what is not defensible. This problem confronts the United States in the early years of the twenty-first century. The American defense budget is now in excess of $500 billion a year. The White House, Congress and the Pentagon all play roles in determining American military doctrine.

According to the doctrine currently in force, the United States military, in addition to securing the homeland, must be capable of winning two major wars at the same time in different parts of the world. And all of this must be done while sustaining American guard duty on the frontiers of the empire in places like the South Korean frontier with North Korea, or the maintenance of US defense establishments in Japan and Germany.

The problem is that despite its enormous power, the US military has been stretched thin in recent years with the invasion and occupation of Iraq. With regular forces unable to do the full job, National Guard reserve units have been called up for lengthy overseas duty. Men and women who joined the National Guard to further their education now find themselves serving in Iraq for long stints, something they never thought they would have to do.

The burden of the military budget is being felt by the United States at a time of mounting economic crisis indicated by flashing warning signals. The US military budget was dramatically increased to pay for the Bush administration's invasions of Afghanistan and Iraq at the same time as the administration's other key policy, a major tax cut aimed mainly at the well-to-do, was taking effect. The combination of the two, along with the effects of an economic slowdown, propelled the US government from the surplus it enjoyed at the end of the Clinton presidency to a rapidly mounting deficit, which reached over $500 billion in 2004. Given the insistence on combining expensive overseas military operations with cheap government, there was no reasonable prospect that the deficit could be eliminated. As a consequence, the US government faced a rising debt, which was fast approaching $8 trillion, on which interest payments had to be made.

To finance the alarming gap between money collected in taxes by the US government and money spent, the United States relied ever more on the sale of treasury bills to foreigners. Between them, China and Japan held over $1 trillion worth of US treasury bills. Dependence on foreigners, and in the case of China, the Chinese government, for capital to keep the American government financially afloat, made the United States dangerously vulnerable to pressures from abroad. In a dispute with China — we will have more to say about US-Chinese rivalry — the US would be susceptible to a Chinese decision to cease its purchase of US treasury bills, an act that would have a seriously destabilizing effect on interest rates in the United States and on the stability of the US dollar.[1]

The spectacular rise of the US government deficit reflects a basic contradiction in the government's approach that is rooted in American political attitudes. George W. Bush's Republican Party, the party that supports a foreign policy that involves high-risk military interventions along with a minimum reliance on America's traditional alliances, is also the low-tax party in the United States. For the past couple of decades, as the Republican Party has become the voice of neo-conservatism in the United States, it has promoted the idea that low taxation and the reduction of the power of Washington in relation to the states will promote entrepreneurship and rapid economic growth. The clash between a high military budget and low taxes is readily

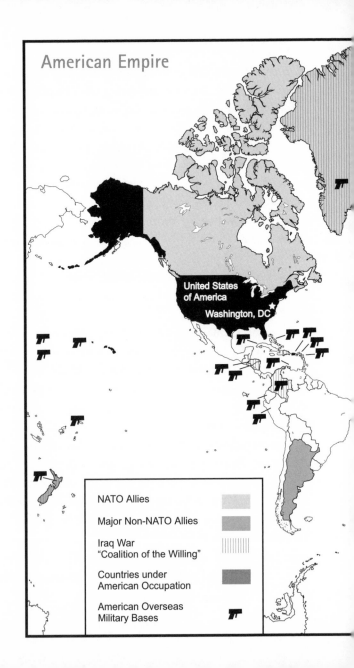

American Empire

United States
of America

Washington, DC

NATO Allies

Major Non-NATO Allies

Iraq War
"Coalition of the Willing"

Countries under
American Occupation

American Overseas
Military Bases

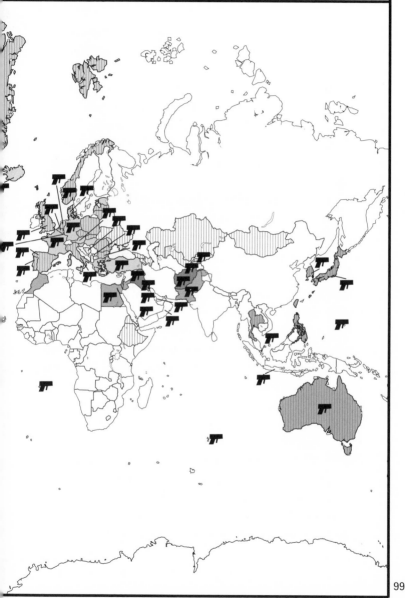

apparent. Both under Ronald Reagan and George W. Bush that clash in thinking has led to huge government deficits.

What is involved is more than a mix of incompatible policies at the governmental level. The contradiction is deeply rooted in American political culture. In the United States, the so-called "red states" (the Republican Party's color), which predominantly vote for George W. Bush, are strongly committed to the goal of lower taxes. For the Republican Party to back away from such a policy stance would risk a political rupture and a loss of support. The red states are also those most remote from the influences of the wider world. They are home to a strong American nationalism that is suspicious of foreign influences and that traditionally can be described as hospitable to isolationist ideas.

Here we encounter a vast irony. The culture of the segment of America that most supports George W. Bush and the Republicans is also the segment that least wants involvement with the rest of the world. And yet this is the political base for an aggressive foreign policy and for the invasions of Afghanistan and particularly Iraq. To make sense of the riddle, it is necessary to understand that the combination of aggressiveness and isolationism is deeply rooted in American thinking, going right back to the American Revolution. Even before the revolution, Americans thought of themselves as a special people, endowed with a godly mission. According to this idea, the US constituted a City on a Hill that served as a beacon, a shining example to all other peoples. (The oft-repeated metaphor comes from a speech by Puritan John Winthrop in 1630, based on Matthew 5:14: "You are the light of the world. A city on a hill cannot be hidden."[2]) Convinced of the mission of their country in the world, it was natural enough for Americans both to want to guard the qualities that made their country unique and to bestow the benefits of Americanism on other peoples.

The notion of the US as a special nation, superior to others in its virtue and achievements, has served as the ideological underpinning of American imperialism. Previous empires have also required the development of notions that justify their interventions abroad. For the British, it was self-evident that they were taking the ways of civilization to other, lesser peoples, or to use Rudyard Kipling's phrase, they were bearing "the white man's burden." Similarly, the Romans conceived of their empire as both a universal and an eternal state, within whose boundaries civilization existed, as opposed to the barbarian mores of those beyond the frontiers.

Those most imbued with this strain of American thinking, the residents of the red states, are prepared to fight wars abroad to counter threats to American security and the American way of life. Such people are not easily won over to any notion of conquest for the sake of conquest. And American leaders have never pitched the need for foreign wars to Americans in those terms. The

Korean and Vietnam wars were justified as wars that were necessary to protect Americans by halting the advance of communism. The invasion of Afghanistan in 2001 was justified as a direct retaliation against the base from which the attacks on New York City and Washington, DC had come. The invasion of Iraq was explained by President Bush as necessary on the grounds that Saddam Hussein's regime was developing weapons of mass destruction that could be used in a sudden assault on the United States. US Secretary of State Condoleezza Rice warned that failing an attack on Iraq, the first sign Americans might have of Hussein's weapons program might come in the form of a mushroom cloud over an American city.

If aggressiveness, isolationism and a belief in low taxation form essential ingredients in the political culture of the red states, the political culture of states that vote for the Democrats (blue states) is different in some important respects. While residents of the blue states generally accept the basic idea of the United States as a special nation with a mission to perform, they are less hostile to foreign states and cultures. And they are much more open to the notion that America needs allies to perform its global tasks. The culture of the blue states is more multilateralist (willing to work with other nations) and less isolationist. Residents of these states have been alarmed by the invasion of Iraq, fearing that it could lead America into a hopeless quagmire, a quagmire made more intractable because the US lacks the backing of the United Nations and of many traditional US allies.

Broadly speaking, the residents of the blue states are less hostile to the idea of higher taxes and are more alarmed by the prospect of US government deficits than are their red-state counterparts. It is not, however, the case that the blue states have a political culture that rejects the idea of the special US mission in the world. Rather than seeing the political culture of red states and blue states as dramatically opposed to one another, it helps to think of a continuum of American views from multilateralist to unilateralist, a spectrum that is rather narrow despite the heated debates that sometimes occur.

The American Empire, despite the omission of the word empire to describe it, is broadly supported by all significant streams of American political thought. What divides the streams is how to sustain the empire and promote its long-term interests. The problem of financing the empire, made worse with the Republicans in power, is a long-term dilemma that confronts the American political leadership whether Democrats or Republicans occupy the White House. Previous empires, notably the Roman and the French, came to grief precisely because of the unwillingness of their upper classes to pay the taxes that would have kept their states intact. Whether Americans, with their strong preference for immediate economic gratification, can be convinced to bear the burden of paying to defend their empire, is one of the great questions that faces the United States in this century.

Another great question is how effectively America will stand up to imperial challengers in the coming decades. At present, the most active challenge to American power comes from the Islamic world. It is not unlikely, however, that the greatest challenge will come from the rise of China. The problems that face the United States in the Islamic world are largely, though not exclusively, the consequence of the position adopted by the United States in the Middle East. Since the late 1940s, it has been a premise of American foreign policy, whichever party has occupied the White House, that the United States must retain strategic control of the Persian Gulf. Around the narrow waters of the Persian Gulf are a number of key countries, whose significance is heavily based on the fact that this region is the vital center of world petroleum reserves and production. Saudi Arabia is home to the world's largest petroleum reserves, reserves that can be brought into production at the lowest prices. Iran and Iraq also hold immense reserves, as do a number of smaller states around the Gulf, including Kuwait. A petroleum-based, industrial civilization for the past century, the United States has long been unable to produce enough oil and natural gas to meet its domestic needs. While its largest sources of imported petroleum are Canada, Mexico and Venezuela, the United States recognizes the Persian Gulf region as having immense significance for Europe, Asia and, not a small matter, the major multinational petroleum companies that are head-quartered in the United States. From the American point of view, allowing the Persian Gulf region to fall into the hands of a hostile power, or a combination of hostile powers, is not to be contemplated.

Prior to the invasion of Iraq, the traditional American policy was to maintain a strong alliance with the authoritarian Saudi Arabian regime. Fears about the long-term viability of the Saudi royal government and concerns about the rise of anti-American feeling in Saudi Arabia motivated American thinkers with close ties to the Bush administration to conclude that the US should not put all its strategic eggs in the Saudi basket. One of the principle reasons for the US invasion of Iraq in 2003, in spite of the justifications used by the Bush administration about Saddam's weapons of mass destruction, was the US desire to stake out a new base in the Persian Gulf. From Iraq, went the thinking of people like Paul Wolfowitz, Deputy Secretary of State, the US would be in a position to keep a wary eye on neighboring Saudi Arabia as well as on Iran and Syria, all countries that border Iraq. Wolfowitz was influential in convincing the administration that if the US toppled Saddam's regime, Iraq could be remodeled as a client US state with a political culture highly amenable to US values. Iraq could be an Islamic country in which a non-fundamentalist outlook could take root, anchored in an American-style democratic system of government. Not least, the United States could establish long-term military bases in Iraq, and US oil companies could achieve a lock on Iraqi oil fields, dislodging competitors from France and Russia.

The initial hopes that accompanied the invasion soon vanished. Americans and their allies were not welcomed as liberators in Iraq, especially in the Sunni heartland of the country around Baghdad. As the months passed, a highly potent, armed insurgency challenged the occupiers. Over the first three years of the occupation, an estimated 35,000 to 98,000 Iraqi civilians have died as a consequence, nearly half of them killed by the Americans and their allies.[3] The long-term outlook for the American intervention in Iraq is far from bright.

The other major policy stance that has embroiled the United States with the Arab and Islamic peoples of the world is American support for Israel in its conflict with the Palestinians. Not only has the United States, whichever party has occupied the White House, poured billions of dollars every year into aid for Israel, the US has stood by Israel amid mounting opposition around the world to Israel's occupation of the West Bank.

Whatever the outcome, it is reasonable to assume that the US stance in the Middle East will continue to require the country to expend blood and treasure for a considerable time. And during this period Americans will be repeatedly concerned with the dangers of terror attack both at home and abroad.

Beyond the issues that embroil the American Empire in the Middle East, there is the looming question of whether the United States can remain essentially unchallenged as the central global power over the next few decades. This question turns principally on an assessment of the significance of the rise of China, and other Asian powers, for the global system of power. With a population of well over one billion people and an economy that has experienced explosive growth, China is a coming global power. In terms of overall economic output, it is likely that China's economy will surpass that of the United States and the even larger output of the European Union in the next quarter century.

Not far behind in economic output will be India, with its population of one billion people, a population that is growing more rapidly than that of China. Overall economic output, it should be pointed out, is not the only significant measure of economic power. The technological lead of the United States, both in terms of the development of new techniques and in terms of the economic literacy of its workforce, can be expected to last considerably longer. But that lead also can be expected to shrink. The rise of a technological workforce in segments of Indian society in recent years is evidence of how things are changing rapidly on this front as well.

Is China likely to become a country with aspirations to establish an empire of its own, an empire undoubtedly centered in Asia, but whose power would be felt all over the world? With its long imperial history, and its sense of itself as a great country and civilization, China certainly has some of the qualities of a potential imperial power. During the days when China was an empire, the Chinese leadership developed the concept of China as the "middle kingdom," the notion that the empire was at the center and that other countries and societies were on the periphery. The notion is similar to the idea the Romans had of their empire as a universal state surrounded by barbarians, or the American idea of the United States as a city on a hill, a special country with a God-given mission to perform.

China is no longer torn by feuding warlords, or forced to grant concessions to the great powers of the West, or the victim of a Japanese war of aggression that lasted over a decade and killed twenty million Chinese. United, free from external occupation, prosperous and rising as a great economic power, Chinese progress has generated a potent nationalism that is often directed against the United States, and recently has been directed against Japan, and any effort that country might make to gain a permanent seat on the United Nations Security Council. With the tacit approval of the Chinese government, a campaign has been waged in China against Japanese unwillingness to acknowledge fully the extent of Japan's crimes in China during the war, and to educate the young in Japan about these atrocities.

With a dictatorial government under the firm control

of the Communist Party, China has crushed movements for democracy, repressed religious rights, and stamped out the efforts of Tibetans and other minority peoples within the country to seek autonomy or independence. Having re-acquired Hong Kong in 1997, China is deeply committed to its campaign to impose control over Taiwan as a province of China. The Chinese insistence that other countries not accord diplomatic recognition to Taiwan has been overwhelmingly successful. The United States, for instance, recognizes China as one country, of which Taiwan is a part, but insists that the Taiwanese have a right to decide on their own political course. In addition, the United States has sold advanced weapons systems to Taiwan and the US navy patrols the Taiwan Strait, the waterway between Taiwan and the mainland, insisting that it would help repel any Chinese military assault on the breakaway province. The government in Beijing has warned that any move on the part of the government in Taipei to declare independence would be met by a military invasion.

Prior to the terror attacks on New York City and Washington, DC on September 11, 2001, most global analysts warned that the next major international showdown would likely be a test of power between the United States and China. While US involvement in the Middle East has pushed the China question to one side, the issue has not gone away. Over the status of Taiwan, or over other questions, there is bound to be a process of adjustment in the relationship between the United States and China. That process will not occur in isolation. Intimately involved with it will be the roles and claims of the other great Asian powers, India, Japan, Indonesia and Russia. Over the course of history, rapid changes in power relationships have provoked tension and have often led to major wars. At the center of the coming test of power will be two countries, the United States and China, both of which have a strong sense of their rightful place in the world. And this sense permeates not only the leadership of these countries but their populations as well.

It has been commonplace for analysts of America's global position to regard the fate of the American Empire as something that will be decided in the struggle for power in Eurasia, the world's central land mass on which over two-thirds of the world's population reside. The relationship between the United States and the other countries of the Western Hemisphere is often casually ignored in these discussions. Since 1823, with the proclamation of the Monroe Doctrine, the United States has regarded the Western Hemisphere as its regional backyard, a part of the world in which the US has a natural claim to a sphere of influence. In recent years, however, major Latin American countries, now all formally democracies, have been asserting greater autonomy from the United States, economically and politically. The US campaign to establish a Free Trade Area of the Americas

(FTAA), an extension of the North American Free Trade Area (NAFTA), to the whole hemisphere, minus Cuba, has run into increasing trouble. Brazil, Argentina and Venezuela are among the countries whose governments are resistant to the American model of a free enterprise economy with limited government intervention. A large number of Latin American countries have suffered as a consequence of economic programs imposed by the International Monetary Fund that have resulted in lower living standards and reduced social and educational spending. Not only has Latin America elected reform and left-of-center governments that do not see eye to eye with Washington on economic issues, the region has become less compliant with the United States on broader global questions. Both Mexico and Chile, then members of the UN Security Council, refused to support the US invasion of Iraq in 2003. In addition to its concerns about the direction of Latin American governments, the United States has become alarmed at China signing major trade deals with countries in the region, especially the oil deal with Venezuela, whose president, Hugo Chavez, has been locked in a major power struggle with the United States.

To this list of regions of the world where challenges are on the horizon for the American Empire, it must be noted that the European Union, with its twenty-five member countries and a population of 480 million people, is an economic power that threatens US leadership

The Price of Empire

In June 2001, the US Congress authorized President George W. Bush's tax cut, valued at $1.35 trillion over the coming decade. That tax cut has led to a sharp drop in US federal tax revenue, from 21 percent to 16 percent of the US Gross Domestic Product (GDP). In 2000, there was a budget surplus of $236 billion, and the total debt of the US government stood at $5.7 trillion; by 2004, the surplus had morphed into a $520 billion deficit, and the debt had grown to a colossal $7.4 trillion.

Since the end of the Cold War at the beginning of the 1990s, American defense spending has followed two distinct trends. For the period 1991 to 2001, it remained relatively constant, fluctuating between $265 billion and $304 billion, and annually representing roughly 16 percent of overall US federal spending. Since 2001, both in terms of total dollars and as a percentage of federal allocations, spending on defense has risen by approximately $50 billion a year, and the total defense expenditure for 2005 was on track to reach $500 billion, or over 20 percent of overall federal spending.

The United States has 725 official military bases around the world and another 969 at home. In addition to standard army, navy, air force and marine bases at home, the United

in significant ways. Despite the severe problems of the EU in integrating old and new members into the union and winning Europeans over to the concept of a stronger central government and constitution for the EU, the creation of the European single market and the establishment of the Euro as the currency of most of the EU

States deploys more than half a million military personnel, spies and civilian contract employees in other parts of the world. Well known is the Guantanamo naval base in Cuba, which now includes a notorious prison for foreign detainees. Less often thought of as bases but at least as important are the thirteen naval task forces operated by the US Navy on the seas of the world. Tens of thousands of service personnel are on these ships, which are armed with nuclear missiles and jet fighters. In many parts of the world, the United States also operates secret bases, from which so-called black operations, secret missions, are mounted. Reliable reports confirm that prisoners are held incommunicado on these secret bases. Other American military installations are so enormous that the word base does not do them justice. For instance, the US Marine base on Okinawa, Japan's southernmost island, is a virtual US colony in East Asia. No other country in the world has military bases on a scale that remotely compares with those of the United States.

By the end of November 2005, over 2,300 American service men and women had been killed in Iraq since the US invasion of that country in March 2003.

has made it a much more coherent economic power. European regulatory authority now has a strong effect on the global behavior of American-based multinational corporations. With its strong current account surplus and its much less severe problem of government deficits, in comparison with the United States, the Euro area is able to take on the US as a financial leader. The Euro is a definite challenger to the US dollar as a potential global reserve currency.

In addition to the threats to US supremacy from other powers, a threat faces the US and the other industrial powers as a consequence of the environmental degradation that results from the industrialization of such large parts of the world. The United States, during the period of its domination, has been a carbon-based civilization par excellence. Excess use of carbon, scientists agree, threatens the world with catastrophic climate change. In addition, the production of readily available supplies of petroleum (not counting oil sands and oil shales and the liquefaction of coal) is nearing its peak, if that peak has not already been reached. This fact and potential shortages of other basic materials can be expected to exert immense pressures on the United States and the other major industrial powers to adapt to new realities within a narrow time frame. These pressures will undoubtedly call into question the norms and consumption patterns of American civilization and the power relationships within American society and in the American Empire. These challenges may well have as much or more to do with the fate of the American Empire as the pressures from other states.

Chapter 5
Resistance to Empire

Beyond the challenges that face the American Empire in our era, there is the broad question about whether empires are likely to constitute as important a feature of the human landscape in the future as they have over thousands of years, throughout the period of what we can call recorded history. One justification for empire made by champions of American global power is that the world needs a single dominant power in order for a thriving international order and global economy to exist. Without such an empire, or hegemonic power, the argument goes, the world would descend into chaos.

Rivalries between states and the rise of failed states where terrorists and drug dealers and other criminals take root, already pose severe problems for the world. Without a power like the United States to police the international system and to enforce the broadly agreed rules, the world would become much more dangerous, according to the proponents of empire.

Despite the flaws of the American Empire and the problems with the domination of the world by a single power, such people argue, only the US can intervene where intervention is needed to deal with threats to the entire civilized order. And given that the United States is a nation steeped in a tradition of liberty and democracy, it is far better that this power should dominate than to have a leading power with harsher and more autocratic values. The defenders of empire point to the period from 1914 to 1945, when Britain was no longer strong enough to sustain a liberal world system and when the US was not prepared to play that role, as a warning to those who believe the world could do without a dominant power. During that thirty-year period, totalitarian regimes emerged in the Soviet Union, Nazi Germany, fascist Italy and militarist Japan, and the consequence of their challenges for power was the Second World War in which tens of millions of people died.

Half a century ago, as the great European powers were losing their empires, many people hoped that the world was moving beyond empire, a form of rule in which one people imposed its domination over other peoples. With the formation of the United Nations at the end of the Second World War, and with its proclamation of the right of nations to self-government and the right of all human beings to dignity and freedom, it seemed that an alternative course could be possible. Despite the Cold War and the threat of nuclear weapons, it seemed that the idea of the rule of law could be extended to the international sphere.

At the beginning of the twenty-first century, such hopes can be seen as having been premature. The American Empire and its would-be challengers may have invented new imperial forms but the fact of empire has not gone away. Despite the claims made by the defenders of empire in our time, the raw fact is that empires are vast engines of inequality, as much so today as in the past. This book began with the assertion that empire and slavery were simultaneous inventions at the dawn of recorded history. Those who had force at their disposal were able to subject people, both outside their societies and within them, to a system of rule that forced the vast majority of the population to work for a privileged few. While the forms of that rule have changed over the millennia, the content has remained substantially the same. Today's dominant empire has harnessed technology to make it possible to organize almost the whole of the world's population into a global division of labor. For those who live in the advanced countries, it is easy to imagine that most people are pretty well off. Only about 15 percent of the world's population, however, lives in the advanced countries in the so-called first world. And even in these countries, there is widespread poverty and only a small proportion of the population is rich. The overwhelming majority of the people who live in the other 85 percent of the world's countries are poor, and a high percentage of those are destitute. The dominant empire oversees the arrangements that maintain this system of global power. In most of the so-called third world, tiny elites, tied tightly to the power of the United States, oversee the exploitation of their own people.

That empire remains a stark fact of life in the early years of the twenty-first century does not mean that the dream of a world based on the equality of peoples, and on fairer and more equitable human development of a kind that can be sustained environmentally, is a dream we should abandon.

If one perennial human story for thousands of years has been the rise and fall of empires, the other side of that story has been the resistance to empires. Empires are, and have always been, about inequality, about the imposition of rule by one people over others. And human beings have never been prepared to settle for a permanent condition of inequality and domination. Resistance to empire has sometimes involved only a few people in particular historical periods. At other times, it has involved the armed struggles of millions of people.

Those who were taken into slavery by the early empires fought back against their condition when the opportunity arose. One of the most famous cases of slave resistance came in the first century BC, when a slave revolt in Italy, led by the slave and gladiator Spartacus, very nearly overturned the rising Roman Empire. For a time, nearly all of Italy fell under the control of Spartacus and his army of slaves. In the end, the Roman military triumphed over the revolt. As many as six thousand slaves met their deaths nailed to crosses along the Roman road, the Appian Way.[1]

As in the case of the bloody suppression of Spartacus and his followers, ruling regimes have put down slave revolts with great severity. Nothing has filled the hearts and minds of the rulers of empires with as much dread as the prospect of a revolt of the slaves who provide the manpower to sustain the system. During the two and a half centuries when slavery existed in the thirteen colonies and the United States, slave revolts, although often neglected in standard histories of the US, were much more common than popularly thought. What was probably the largest slave revolt in American history occurred near New Orleans in 1811. Between four and five hundred slaves assembled after a struggle at a plantation. Armed with primitive weapons, they marched from plantation to plantation gathering recruits. When they were met by US army and militia units, sixty-six of the rebels were killed at once. Sixteen more were tried and executed. In 1822, an audacious conspiracy led by Denmark Vesey, a free black, planned the burning of Charleston, South Carolina, to be followed by a general slave uprising throughout the region. The conspiracy was thwarted and thirty-five blacks, including Vesey, were executed.[2]

One successful slave revolt against a major European

empire was the struggle of Haitians to free themselves from French rule. Ninety percent of the people of Haiti, formerly called Saint-Domingue, were black slaves, who worked on the plantations of the island, which made this France's most profitable colony during the eighteenth century. The slave rebellion began in August 1791 and continued until the struggle was won with the achievement of the independence of Haiti in 1804. The most prominent leader to emerge from the struggle was Toussaint L'Ouverture, a former slave, who organized and led armies that defeated Spanish and British forces. In 1801, Napoleon Bonaparte sent a French army numbering thousands of men to suppress the Haitian revolution. Toussaint was tricked by the French, captured and sent to France, where he died in prison in 1803. Jean-Jacques Dessalines, also a former slave and one of Toussaint's generals, assembled his forces and defeated the French army. On January 1, 1804, he proclaimed Haiti an independent country, the first black republic in the world.

Throughout the centuries of its existence, the British Empire provoked resistance many times in different historical periods. One of the most concerted and tragic struggles against British rule unfolded in Ireland. From the mid-sixteenth century, when the English, later joined by the Scots, began their campaign to rule Ireland, resistance flared and sometimes died out for a time. The Irish struggle continued until the establishment of the Irish

Free State, in the twenty-six counties of southern Ireland, in the early 1920s. Even after that date, in Northern Ireland, which remained a part of the United Kingdom, the Catholic minority continued its quest for equal rights and for Irish unity against the implacable opposition of the dominant local Protestant majority (see The Quest for Irish Freedom, pages 123-29).

Another uprising, which has become a symbol of tragic resistance against a genocidal empire, was the armed struggle of the Jewish inhabitants of the Warsaw Ghetto against the Nazis in April and May 1943. The uprising broke out when reports of the mass killings of Jews who had been sent from the Warsaw Ghetto to Treblinka were received by those who remained in the ghetto. When the Nazis dispatched soldiers and police into the ghetto, 750 Jewish fighters opened fire on the Germans. In the one-sided struggle, the resisters held out for more than a month. In the end, when the Germans crushed the resistance, thousands of the survivors were shot, and the rest were sent to the death camps.

Peaceful resistance to empires, the most famous being Mahatma Gandhi's salt march in 1930 (to mobilize Indians to challenge British authority) and hunger strikes during the struggle for the independence of India, have been a major feature of the politics of the past century. Gandhi's march was designed to show the people of India the absurdity of a British system of rule under which Indians were not allowed to avail themselves of their own salt, readily available, without paying a British tax. From such beginnings, the movement for independence led to the end of British rule on the Indian subcontinent in 1947 (see India's Struggle Against the British Raj, pages 130-35).

In our own time, a movement of young people in the developed world in opposition to the inequities of globalization arose in the late 1990s. Armed with their fierce opposition to global exploitation, the theatrical skills they brought to their demonstrations, and their inspired use of new communications technology, this novel political force soon compelled world leaders to hold their meetings behind steel fences and battalions of police wielding tear gas. On January 19, 2003, weeks before the US invasion of Iraq, ten million people demonstrated in cities around the world against the coming war. It was the greatest mass mobilization for peace ever undertaken.

If empire remains a potent force in our time, the power of those who are determined to resist the sway of empire is the other great fact of our world.

THE QUEST FOR IRISH FREEDOM

One of the longest and most bitter struggles for independence from empire was that waged by the people of Ireland against British rule. The English conquest of Ireland began with King Henry VIII's claim that he was the king of Ireland in 1541. From a small English presence around Dublin in the sixteenth century came complete control of the island in the following century.

Irish resistance to British rule waxed and waned over a period of centuries. In 1800, the Act of Union, which came into effect on January 1, 1801, made Ireland a part of the United Kingdom, which meant that from then on the people of Ireland elected members to the British parliament.

Irish representation in the British House of Commons in the early nineteenth century was dominated by the Anglo-Irish gentry under the extremely narrow franchise of the time, which also applied in England. As the decades passed the franchise was enlarged so that by the late nineteenth century it included the whole adult male population. The Irish National Party came to dominate Ireland's parliamentary caucus at Westminster and evolved a program and a strategy that brought the issue of Irish self-government to the fore of British politics. The program was called Home Rule, a demand for status for Ireland roughly equivalent to that of the British Empire's self-governing dominions such as Canada. The strategy, which only became effective in the 1880s, was to seize an opportunity when the Liberals and Conservatives – the two major parties in British politics – were so closely divided that the Irish nationalists could hold the balance of power in the House of Commons and compel one of the two major parties to adopt their program.

Long before the Irish nationalists became a potent political force in British politics, the lamentable condition of Ireland was there for all to see, at least for those who cared to look. In reality, if not in theory,

Ireland was a British colony, ruled by Anglo-Irish landowners and populated by people who lived, for the most part, in abject poverty. The tragic condition of the population reached its terrible climax in the years following 1849, when the potato famine resulted in a starvation so devastating that the population of whole villages simply died. Even though Britain could have intervened to save hundreds of thousands of people from starvation, very little was done on behalf of the Irish. The mid-nineteenth-century Irish population was halved as a result of the starvation of a million people and the migration of at least another million, principally to the United States and Canada.

It was William Ewart Gladstone, the giant of nineteenth-century British liberalism, who opened the door to the possible achievement of Irish Home Rule during his term as prime minister from 1880 to 1885. Gladstone's initiative plunged his party into a crisis. Within the Liberal Party were forces led by Joseph Chamberlain, the radical, pro-imperialist demagogue who saw the devolution of even modest powers of self-government to Ireland as a grave threat to the survival of the British Empire. As a consequence of divisions within the Liberal Party, among other things, Home Rule remained unrealized when the First World War broke out in 1914.

Since the parliamentary struggle seemed to have gotten them nowhere, the more radical Irish nationalists turned to violence. On Easter Sunday 1916, a band of about one thousand Irish patriots led by the poet Patrick Pearse launched an armed revolt in Dublin. Among their number was the Socialist Labor leader James Connolly, famous for his militant efforts on behalf of working people in Ireland and on the British mainland. The republicans seized the Dublin Post Office and other sites in the center of the capital. Following in the footsteps of patriot leaders in other countries who had declared independence from empire for their peoples, Pearse proclaimed the birth of an Irish republic:

Irishmen and Irishwomen: in the name of God and of the dead generations from which she receives her old tradition of nationhood, Ireland, through us, summons her children to her flag, and strikes for her freedom....We hereby proclaim the Irish Republic as a Sovereign Independent State, and we pledge our lives and the lives of our comrades-at-arms to the cause of its freedom, its welfare, and of its exaltation among the nations."[3]

The uprising came as a shock to the British, who were embroiled in France in the vicious trench warfare of the First World War against Germany. They responded by rushing troops across the Irish Sea from England. For three days the fighting continued, with the British shelling rebel positions with artillery shells that demolished a portion of central Dublin. Forced to withdraw from the post office, Pearse decided he had no option but to surrender. When the firing stopped, sixty-four Irish rebels and one hundred and thirty British soldiers were dead. With the exception of a few limited actions elsewhere in the country, the popular rising of the Irish people on which the rebels had counted had not taken place.

Between May 3 and 10, following swift British courts-martial, fifteen of the rebels were shot, executed in groups of two or three. Wounded during the uprising, James Connolly was court-martialed in his bed and was borne, tied to a chair, to his place of execution. Pearse and his brother Willie were also shot. At his court-martial, Pearse defiantly predicted that the cause of Irish independence would endure:

We seem to have lost. We have not lost....You cannot conquer Ireland, you cannot extinguish the Irish passion for freedom. If our deed has not been sufficient to win freedom, then our children will win it with a better deed.[4]

More potent in death than during their rebellion, the martyrs of the Easter uprising became symbols of the viciousness of British rule. The majority of Irish Catholics had not rallied to Pearse's call to arms, but they were sickened by the vengeful response of the British. Although relatively few had died in the armed struggle in Dublin, in comparison with other campaigns for national independence, the British position in Ireland never recovered.

After the rebellion, Home Rule was a concept whose time had passed. Republicanism, a complete break with the British Empire, was what the nationalists now demanded. Following a failed attempt to negotiate a deal between nationalists and Protestant unionists, who wanted to stay in the United Kingdom, Sinn Fein (Ourselves Alone), the new party of the nationalists, emerged as the predominant voice of Irish freedom. With the British overwhelmingly focused on winning the war against the Germans in France, the British administration of Ireland, headquartered at Dublin Castle, began to lose its ability to govern the country. The seismic shift in Irish sentiment was revealed in the results of the British general election of December 1918. In Ireland, Sinn Fein won 76 seats (47 of those elected were in jail), and the Unionists took 26 seats, while only six Home Rule advocates were elected. A month after the election, the Sinn Fein MPs assembled in Dublin and proclaimed the establishment of the Republic of Ireland, with Eamon de Valera as its president. Acting through the Dail Eireann (the Irish parliament newly created by Sinn Fein), the government set about the task of creating an administration of its own to challenge the authority of the British administration.

During the "time of troubles" that continued for the next two years, the militants of the Irish Republican Army (IRA), dressed in civilian clothing, waged a guerilla war against the Royal Irish Constabulary (police force) and the British army, carrying out murderous assaults on them and then blending back into the Irish population on the streets. On a number of occasions, they carried out large-scale, well-coordinated attacks on police stations and other British installations. In retaliation, the British struck back, not only at the IRA men, when they could get their hands on them, but they frequently vented their fury on the local population.

As the ugly war raged, the British government came up with a formula for achieving peace with the passage of a bill in parliament in the spring of 1920. The Irish Home Rule bill was to partition Ireland into two states, the twenty-six counties with Catholic majorities in the south, and the six counties with Protestant majorities in the north. There would be parliaments in Dublin and Belfast, but foreign and defense policies would remain firmly in the hands of the British.

Sinn Fein rejected the British plan and the war continued with de Valera touring the United States, where he was feted as a hero by Irish-Americans. In the US, he raised funds to sustain the Irish cause, and behind the scenes, he acquired money to purchase arms for the IRA fighters. On their side, the British recruited a brutish army, mostly composed of ex-servicemen, in places such as London, Glasgow and Birmingham. These infamous members of the Black and Tans, as they were dubbed, replaced the regular police in large parts of the country. They were notorious for their brutal attacks on civilian non-combatants and were seen by the Irish people as an army of occupation.

Tit-for-tat massacres reached a deadly climax on November 21, 1920, when IRA men gunned down twelve British military officers, claiming that they were intelligence agents. The same afternoon, members of the Royal Irish Constabulary Auxiliary opened fire on spectators at a Dublin football match, later claiming they were returning the fire of IRA gunmen. Twelve were shot dead or were crushed to death by the fleeing spectators.

In October 1921, the British government opened peace talks with Sinn Fein and the two sides reached an agreement in early December. Under the terms of the Anglo-Irish Treaty, the twenty-six counties of the south became a dominion in the British Empire, known as the Irish Free State. The treaty also stipulated that the six counties of the north, in Protestant Ulster, were to be carved out of Ireland and were to remain in the United Kingdom. In addition, Ulster was to have its own local parliament.

Through the treaty, most of Catholic Ireland won self-government. But the treaty divided the nationalists into two bitterly opposed camps. The pragmatists, who were led by de Valera, reasoned that they had won as much as they could get from the British, and that they would have to accept a deal that kept them in the British Empire, for a time at least. They also concluded that they did not have the strength to block the partition of Ireland, which would have pitted them against the British army and the militant fighters of the Ulster loyalists. In the Irish Dail, de Valera's side carried the day in favor of the treaty by a margin of only seven votes. The hardliners refused to live with the result. For them, the partition of Ireland was seen as the betrayal of a sacred cause. A new armed conflict erupted between the pragmatists and these hardliners. De Valera and the pragmatists prevailed, but not before the fighting crossed the border into Ulster, which led in turn to violent reprisals against the Catholic minority in Ulster.

In 1949, Ireland seceded from the Commonwealth. Citizens of the Irish Republic retained the right to migrate freely to the UK. The tragic Irish struggles did not end with the establishment of an independent Irish state, however. In the north, armed conflict erupted in the 1970s. On one side were the Catholic nationalists, who fought to end what they saw as the unequal treatment of the Catholic minority in Ulster and to finish the job of creating a united and independent Ireland that would be governed from Dublin. On the other side were the Ulster Protestant loyalists, who were determined to keep the north in the United Kingdom and to sustain Protestant supremacy in their corner of Ireland. While the armed conflict has come to an end in the north, with the Catholic and Protestant militias disarming, the struggle to shape the future of Ulster is far from finished.

The Irish won their freedom, but the legacy of empire is not so easily relegated to the past. As in other parts of the world, the consequences of British rule included the establishment of a settler faction, the Protestants in Ulster, who fought bitterly in opposition to the efforts of nationalists to achieve independence for their homeland. Today the context in which the Irish struggle continues is dramatically different from the situation in the 1920s. The British Empire is no more and both the Irish Republic and the United Kingdom are members of a new federation, the European Union. Ireland has thrived economically in the EU and there is hope that in the wider setting of Europe, ways can be found for Ireland's multiple identities to be preserved in a democratic setting that at last can transcend the desperate battles of the past.

INDIA'S STRUGGLE AGAINST THE BRITISH RAJ

The struggle of the people of India for independence from the British Empire eerily echoed the campaigns of the Irish for their freedom. While Ireland was Britain's first colony, India was the jewel of the empire, the homeland of no fewer than 80 percent of the inhabitants of the British Empire. Following the British suppression of the great Indian rebellion of 1857, which continued for many months, the struggle for Indian freedom took a different course. In the end, it was the building of one of history's most remarkable mass movements that led the people of India to their goal.

As was the case with the British response to the Easter rebellion in Ireland in 1916, a British massacre in India in 1919 was a seminal event in hardening the population's determination to achieve national independence. The massacre occurred at Amritsar, the holy city of the Sikhs in the Punjab on April 3. Under orders from Brigadier-General R.E.H. Dyer, Indian army troops fired on a crowd of about 20,000 demonstrators who were protesting peacefully for wider political rights. The demonstrators were enclosed within a walled area whose gates had been locked on British orders. The firing continued for twenty minutes until at last Dyer called it to a halt. Nearly 400 Indians were killed and more than 1,000 wounded.

Horror at the massacre and the public floggings that followed it was felt throughout India and the whole of the British Empire. An imperial commission of inquiry, while reprimanding Dyer for not warning the demonstrators at Amritsar to disperse and for not providing medical aid to the wounded, ended by taking no legal action against the commander. Dyer, although forced to take early retirement on half pay, received his army pension.

For some British observers, Dyer was a hero, standing up for law and order at Amritsar. The writer Maud Diver spoke for many of her countrymen, both at home and in India, when she wrote:

Organized revolt is amenable only to the ultimate argument of force. Nothing, now, would serve but strong action and the compelling power of martial law.... At Amritsar strong action had already been taken.... The sobering effect of it spread in widening circles, bringing relief to thousands of both races.[5]

By the time of the atrocity at Amritsar, Mahatma Gandhi had already become one of the chief leaders of the Indian nationalist movement. His response to the massacre was to state that further cooperation with this "satanic regime" was impossible. Gandhi had been educated in England and called to the bar in London. He had learned his political skills in South Africa where he spent two decades leading the struggle of its Indian population against discrimination. By the time he returned to India in 1915, he had evolved a strategy for the liberation of the subcontinent that was completely at variance with the approach taken by other English-educated Indian leaders.

Gandhi's plan was to mobilize a mass movement of a kind the world had never seen, a movement that would confront the well-armed British with peaceful, but determined non-violent resistance. His chosen method of struggle was *satyagraha*, which he translated as meaning "soul force" or "love force." This described a state of being that enabled a person to develop the inner strength, faith and determination to resist an unjust regime through non-violent means.

His calculation was that although the British could easily meet force with superior force, they could not cope with the non-violent withdrawal of cooperation. Gandhi recognized that Britain's rule of India's vast population with only a small force of Britons could only continue through the willing collaboration of Indians in every field of life, from the military to the administration of the government to the running of the economy. Take that collaboration away and the whole seemingly impervious system of the British Raj would come tumbling down, Gandhi believed.

By 1906, Gandhi in the midst of his struggles in South Africa, had abandoned Western dress, renouncing materialism and most physical pleasures in favor of a life of simplicity in all things. The British found themselves face to face with a charismatic leader who unleashed a spiritual and political force of a kind they found difficult to counter.

In March 1930, Gandhi launched his best-known campaign, whose climax was the Dandi Salt March, designed to mobilize Indians in defiance of the absurdity of the British administration's salt monopoly, which forced Indians to pay a tax on salt. Gandhi's march ended with thousands of Indians marching to the sea and breaking the law simply by picking up the salt that was there for the taking.

Indian nationalism amounted to much more than Gandhi's campaigns, crucial as they were. The Congress movement and later the Congress Party were the great political creations of the Indian movement for self-government. Jawaharlal Nehru, like Gandhi educated in England, emerged as the paramount leader of this movement, which had its roots in the half-million villages of India.

In the face of Indian campaigns for self-government, the strategy of the British government was one of slow retreat. Indians were recruited in greater numbers into the top echelons of the administration, although the most sensitive jobs, those concerned with justice, police and finance, remained in the hands of appointees from Britain. In 1935, a massive reform was made with the passage of the Government of India Act, which introduced major elements of responsible government into the running of the provinces of India, while the central administration continued largely under the control of the British. The Congress Party was the major winner in the provincial elections that followed.

The reform of the mid-1930s ended by satisfying no one, not the nationalists who were determined to achieve full self-government, and not the imperialist diehards who believed that the British Empire was now on the slippery slope to dissolution. The Second World War intervened before India achieved independence, a war in which the soldiers of the subcontinent contributed mightily to the imperial war effort, a war in which India itself was threatened with Japanese invasion.

As in the case of Ireland, the campaign for self-government was deeply compromised by internal conflicts within India itself. During the early days of the political struggle for Indian self-government, most Muslims had been supporters of the Congress Party, with only a minority of them backing the exclusively Muslim political party, the Muslim League. As time passed, however, the sentiment grew among many Muslims that the goal of the Congress Party was to establish a Hindu Raj in place of the British Raj.

As it became clear that Britain was indeed going to transfer full governmental authority to the people of India, the crucial question on the agenda was whether there would be one state or two. Elections in 1945 measured the strength of the Congress Party – which hoped to win enough Muslim support to block the move toward the creation of a separate Muslim state – against that of the Muslim League, which was committed to the establishment of a separate state to be called Pakistan. In the elections to India's central assembly, in which a portion of the seats were set aside for Muslim voters, the Muslim League polled a striking 86.6 percent of the vote. In the races for control of provincial governments, Congress gained control in eight of the eleven provinces, with the Muslim League able to govern in two, and Congress coming to power in a coalition government in the Punjab. Even in the provinces with majority Muslim populations, the Muslim League polled less than half the votes.

Despite the mixed results in the voting, there was a clear standoff between the Congress Party and the Muslim League. While Britain's Labour Government, under the leadership of Clement Attlee, continued to dither about how to complete the final transfer of power to the people of the subcontinent, violence in India played a huge role in setting the agenda. With partition in the offing, millions of Muslims and Hindus moved, in the case of Muslims to territory that would become Pakistan, in the case of Hindus, into areas that would stay a part of India. During the vast upheaval, 250,000 to 600,000 refugees died, the victims of sectarian violence.

What pushed the British government toward a final settlement were a series of mutinies of military personnel in India in 1946. The first and most surprising of these was a mutiny among British servicemen in the Royal Air Force who were unhappy about the very slow pace of repatriation to England and post-war demobilization. Later, personnel in the Indian Air Force and navy carried out their own mutinies in Bombay (now Mumbai), Calcutta (now Kolkata), Madras (now Chennai) and Karachi (now in Pakistan).

The British government sent a mission to India to work out the details of the transfer of power. While the members of the mission considered schemes to avoid the partition of the subcontinent into two states, the strong stand taken by the Muslim League decided the issue.

On August 15, 1947, not one but two new dominions were established: a vast Indian state, with a majority Hindu population, and a very considerable Muslim minority and a smaller Pakistan, which was overwhelmingly Muslim. For its part, Pakistan was cut into two, with West and East Pakistan separated from each other by 1,600 kilometers (994 miles) of Indian territory. (In the early 1970s, East Pakistan achieved independence and became Bangladesh.)

In a radio broadcast to the people of his country, Jawaharlal Nehru,

India's first prime minister, declared that "a moment comes, which comes but rarely in history, when we step out from the old to the new, when an age ends, and when the soul of a nation long suppressed finds utterance."[6]

In January 1948, Gandhi was shot dead, the victim of a plot by Hindu extremists who were deeply opposed to his rejection of violence and his campaign to overcome sectarian hatred.

As was the case for Ireland, the legacy of the past creates grave problems for the subcontinent. India and Pakistan confront each other warily especially in Kashmir, a territory that both sides claim. In Kashmir, Indian and Pakistani forces face each other along a de facto frontier that has often been a flashpoint for fighting. Adding to the problem in our time is the fact that both India and Pakistan have become nuclear powers. While tensions have eased somewhat between the two states, the risk of a nuclear showdown between these two heirs to the British Raj makes this one of the world's greatest danger spots.

Timeline: The Duration of Selected Empires

| | 3000 BC | | | | | | | | | 2000 BC | | | | | | | | | 1000 BC | | |

1. Egyptian Empire • 3000 BC – 30 BC

2. Roman Empire
   • Founding of the Roman Republic, 509 BC
   • Sack of Rome by the Visigoths, AD 410

3. First Han Chinese Empire • 206 BC – AD 25

4. Aztec Empire • 1428 – 1519

5. Inca Empire • 1438 – 1532

6. Spanish Empire

7. Russian Empire • 1462 – 1917

8. French Empire • 1524 – 1962

9. English (later British) Empire • 1576 – 1968

10. Soviet Empire • 1917 – 1991

11. Nazi Germany (Third Reich) • 1933 – 1945

12. The United States

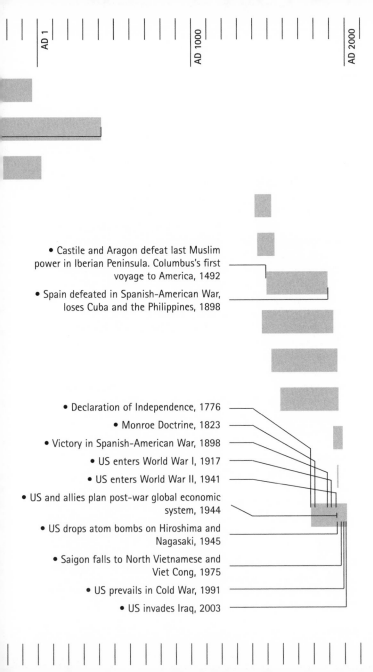

AD 1

AD 1000

AD 2000

• Castile and Aragon defeat last Muslim power in Iberian Peninsula. Columbus's first voyage to America, 1492

• Spain defeated in Spanish-American War, loses Cuba and the Philippines, 1898

• Declaration of Independence, 1776

• Monroe Doctrine, 1823

• Victory in Spanish-American War, 1898

• US enters World War I, 1917

• US enters World War II, 1941

• US and allies plan post-war global economic system, 1944

• US drops atom bombs on Hiroshima and Nagasaki, 1945

• Saigon falls to North Vietnamese and Viet Cong, 1975

• US prevails in Cold War, 1991

• US invades Iraq, 2003

Notes

1 What Is an Empire?

1. All the quotes are from Frederick Engels, *Anti-Duhring: Herr Duhring's Revolution in Science* (London: Martin Lawrence, [1877]), 205-207.

2 Past Empires

1. Stan Hendrickx and Pierre Vermeersch, "Prehistory: From the Palaeolithic to the Badarian Culture," in *The Oxford History of Ancient Egypt*, ed. Ian Shaw (Oxford: Oxford University Press, 2002), 35.

2. M. Cary, *A History of Rome: Down to the Reign of Constantine* (London: Macmillan and Co., 1957), 141-212.

3. M. Cary, *A History of Rome*, 281-472.

4. Edward Gibbon, *History of the Decline and Fall of the Roman Empire* (London: Penguin UK, 1996).

5. Jacques Gernet, *A History of Chinese Civilization* (Cambridge: Cambridge University Press, 1982), 103-28.

6. Henry Kamen, *How Spain Became a World Power, 1492-1763* (New York: Harper Collins, 2003), 151-96.

7. Niall Ferguson, *Empire: The Rise and Demise of the British World Order and the Lessons for Global Power* (London: Basic Books, 2002), 3-58.

8. A.J.P. Taylor, *The Struggle for Mastery in Europe: 1848-1918* (London: Oxford University Press, 1957), 532-68.

9. Ian Kershaw, *Hitler, 1936-1945: Nemesis* (London: Allen Lane, Penguin Books, 2000).

3 The American Empire

1. John Strachey, *The End of Empire* (London: Victor Gollancz Ltd., 1959).

2. Niall Ferguson, *Colossus: The Rise and Fall of the American Empire* (London: Allen Lane, Penguin Books, 2004).

3. Joseph S. Nye Jr., *The Paradox of American Power: Why the World's Only Superpower Can't Go It Alone* (New York: Oxford University Press, 2002).

4. Margaret Macmillan, *Paris 1919: Six Months that Changed the World* (New York: Random House, 2001).

5. Ellen Meiskins Wood, *Empire of Capital* (London, New York: Verso, 2003).

6. P.J. Cain and A.G. Hopkins, *British Imperialism, 1688-2000* (London: Pearson Education Ltd., 2001), 107-34.

4 Cracks in the American Imperial Armor

1. The main source for the statistics in this chapter is *The Statistical Abstract of the United States, 2004-2005*, US Department of Commerce, Economics and Statistics Administration, US Census Bureau.
2. The Bible, New International Version.
3. The lower number, based on confirmed reports, is from Iraq Body Count, available at www.iraqbodycount.org, May 2006; the upper estimate is from Les Roberts et al., "Mortality Before and After the 2003 Invasion of Iraq: Cluster Sample Survey," *The Lancet* 364, Issue 9448 (November 20, 2004), 1857-64.

5 Resistance to Empire

1. M. Cary, *A History of Rome*, 365.
2. Howard Zinn, *A People's History of the United States: 1492-Present* (New York: Harper Perennial, 1993), 167-71.
3. Denis Judd, *Empire: The British Imperial Experience from 1765 to the Present* (Phoenix Press, London, 2001), 242.
4. Denis Judd, *Empire*, 243.
5. Denis Judd, *Empire*, 259.
6. Denis Judd, *Empire*, 323.

For Further Reading

Cain, P.J. and A.G. Hopkins. *British Imperialism, 1688-2000*. London: Pearson Education Ltd., 2001.
Cary, M. *A History of Rome: Down to the Reign of Constantine*. London: Macmillan and Co., 1957.
Ferguson, Niall. *Colossus: The Rise and Fall of the American Empire*. London: Allen Lane, Penguin Books, 2004.
Ferguson, Niall. *Empire: The Rise and Demise of the British World Order and the Lessons for Global Power*. London: Basic Books, 2002.

Gernet, Jacques. *A History of Chinese Civilization.* Cambridge: Cambridge University Press, 1982.

Gibbon, Edward. *History of the Decline and Fall of the Roman Empire.* London: Penguin UK, 1996.

Hobson, J.A. *Imperialism.* Ann Arbor: University of Michigan Press, 1965.

Jackson, Alvin. *Home Rule: An Irish History 1800-2000.* London: Phoenix Press, 2004.

James, Lawrence. *The Rise and Fall of the British Empire.* London: Abacus, 1998.

Judd, Denis. *Empire: The British Imperial Experience from 1765 to the Present.* London: Phoenix Press, 2001.

Kamen, Henry. *How Spain Became a World Power, 1492-1763.* New York: Harper Collins, 2003.

Lenin, V.I. *Imperialism: The Highest Stage of Capitalism.* International Publishing Company, 1969.

Macmillan, Margaret. *Paris 1919: Six Months that Changed the World.* New York: Random House, 2001.

Nye, Joseph S. *The Paradox of American Power: Why the World's Only Superpower Can't Go It Alone.* New York: Oxford University Press, 2002.

Shaw, Ian, ed. *The Oxford History of Ancient Egypt.* Oxford: Oxford University Press, 2002.

Strachey, John. *The End of Empire.* London: Victor Gollancz Ltd., 1959.

Taylor, A.J.P. *The Struggle for Mastery in Europe: 1848-1918.* London: Oxford University Press, 1957.

Wood, Ellen Meiskins. *Empire of Capital.* London, New York: Verso, 2003.

Maps drawn by Leon Grek.

Sources: 22, 28-29: © Copyright Euratlas Nüssli–www.euratlas.com, reproduction prohibited, 2006 (0660619146); 37 Minneapolis Institute of Arts, www.artsmia.org; 42-43, 54-55, 98-99 Geoatlas.

Index